THE REMINISCENCE PUZZLE BOOK

ROBIN DYNES

Routledge
Taylor & Francis Group

LONDON AND NEW YORK

'No man can have in his mind a conception of the future, for the future is not yet. But of our conceptions of the past, we make a future.'
(Thomas Hobbes)

First published 1995 by Speechmark Publishing Ltd

Published 2017 by Routledge
2 Park Square, Milton Park, Abingdon, Oxon OX14 4RN
711 Third Avenue, New York, NY 10017, USA

Routledge is an imprint of the Taylor & Francis Group, an informa business

British Library Cataloguing in Publication Data
Dynes, Robin
  Reminiscence Puzzle Book
  I. Title
  793.73

ISBN: 9780863883484 (pbk)

CONTENTS

Robin Dynes is a trained counsellor who has worked in the probation service, a number of psychiatric hospitals and private practice. He currently manages a mental health day centre that provides a wide variety of therapeutic and life-skills groups, including social and creative activities, as well as individual counselling. He has many years of experience in working with groups and with individuals.

Robin is the author of *Creative Games in Groupwork* (1988), *Creative Writing in Groupwork* (1990), *Memory Games for Groups* (1998), *The Non-Competitive Activity Book* (2000) and *Anxiety Management* (2001), all published by Winslow Press/Speechmark Publishing.

Acknowledgements

Photographs reproduced with kind permission from Hulton Deutsch Collection Limited; The Derby, 1935; Inspectors in a small parts factory, 1940s; Elizabeth II's coronation celebrations, 1953; Man on the moon, 1969; Queen Elizabeth II's Silver Jubilee, 1977; Thatcher and Tebbit, 1987; *(Front cover)* European Tour, 1952 and Hattie Jacques.

Who is this book for?

It is primarily intended for use with individuals or groups of older people. However, the puzzles can be enjoyed by most age groups. I have, for example, used them successfully in a mental health day centre and in a multi-purpose rehabilitation centre with group members whose ages range from 20 to 65 years. The group leader must, of course, be careful not to ask questions about periods before individuals were born or which they would have been too young to reasonably be expected to remember. This is important when using this material with any age group or individual.

Using the book

The Reminiscence Puzzle Book is divided into decades and presents a mixture of events, people, entertainment and information about everyday life. The introduction to each decade gives the feel of the period, as do the 'Do You Remember?' sections presented between the puzzles. These can also be used as extra material for additional questions and topics for discussion to prompt personal memories of the period. Each decade contains six puzzles:

Puzzle 1: WHO DID WHAT?

Achievements, sayings or specific events are stated. Participants name the person or persons involved and enlarge on their memory of the subject.

Puzzle 2: SCRAMBLE

This is a puzzle which asks the group to link persons named with a book, film, song, sport or subject (also given) of the decade. The puzzle can be drawn on a board, the page can be photocopied and handed out to each individual, or the information given can be used to present a straight quiz.

Puzzle 3: WHAT HAPPENED?

A place, date and person involved or other information about an event are given. Participants describe what happened.

Puzzle 4: TRUE OR FALSE?

A statement about a person, event or life in the decade is made. People are invited either to agree or to challenge the statement.

Puzzle 5: WHAT'S THE CONNECTION?

A few facts are listed — these can be about people, places, objects or dates. Participants puzzle out what connects them.

Puzzle 6: FAMOUS PEOPLE CROSSWORD

This is a simple crossword. Clues are given across. Correct answers give an additional famous person downwards. All are linked to events, scandals, sport or entertainment of the decade. This is another puzzle which can be drawn on a board, the crossword page can be photocopied as a handout for individuals, or the information can be used to present a straight quiz.

Except for the 'Scramble' and the 'Famous People Crossword', each puzzle starts at the beginning of the decade and works through to the end. Therefore the period is covered systematically.

The puzzles are adaptable to the abilities of individuals and can be made more challenging or easier by giving clues from the additional facts provided. This information also enables group leaders to stimulate discussion and facilitate members of the group in expressing opinions, feelings about various issues and their own personal experience. The emphasis is not intended to be on the puzzle, though this provides a great deal of fun and enjoyment, but on the personal experience of the individual or group members. Thus they are encouraged to express emotion, their own opinions about the events, their life at the time and to associate events with what was happening to them.

Some issues to keep in mind

Being able to identify more with their past achievements and experience can be helpful to older people when they are in situations of loss. Emphasizing the value of life in the past can help cushion the difference between how a person imagines or wishes life would be and how it is. Reminiscence may also stimulate the traditional role of older people as 'storytellers' and preservers of memories. Often, by looking back, we can better understand bad experiences and learn something from them. We may develop a feeling of acceptance and contentment about our experiences.

However, some sensitivity needs to be exercised regarding how far leaders go in stimulating personal experience. A person may become obsessed with particular past events or situations because of the lack of any satisfactory solution to them, or experience continuing feelings of guilt and depression.

A person's present-day mood may also influence memories. If an individual is feeling down, something pleasant which happened in the past may be looked at pessimistically. Alternatively, if a person feels well and comfortable, the past, even if it contains much sadness and hardship, may be viewed in a positive way.

Strength can be gained from the past through a person understanding their experience, connecting events and achieving perspective and a sense of their life direction. But there can be, in some cases, conflict between the past and the present. Some people need to break bonds with their past and begin anew. Others may have been through a period of life review and feel less need to retrace their steps. A person may resist thinking about the past as a defence against something they have difficulty handling, or an inability to overcome a loss through not being able to grieve properly. For most people, it will be helpful to look back. The experience of growing older is different for each person and the group leader needs to be aware of and sensitive to these issues.

Reminiscence is also useful to help leaders or carers understand each individual's way of thinking and seeing the world. People from different backgrounds, generations or social class, with different education and experience, will have vastly different expectations of life and will therefore behave and react differently to what is happening around and to them.

A carer exploring an individual's past with them can help both people understand the situation better, leaving the individual feeling the carer has a better appreciation of them as a human being. Also, carers can spot ways in which people have coped in the past which can be used again.

Using *The Reminiscence Puzzle Book* provides a lot of enjoyment and also enables group members or individuals to look back, view their lives from a distance, obtain perspective and gain a sense of direction. It also assists the carer or group leader in being able to see and understanding each person's view of the world.

the 1930s

THE BEGINNING of the 1930s was dominated by the
effects of the Depression. A slump in world trade,
aggravated by the Wall Street crash in 1929, led to a
financial crisis in 1931. A National Government was
formed to prove to foreign investors that Britain was
sound.

In an emergency budget on 10 September 1931 the standard rate of tax was raised from 4s 6d to 5s 0d in the pound. Allowances for children were reduced and surtax was increased. Government ministers, judges, MPs, the police and the armed services suffered a 10 per cent pay cut. Teachers' wages were reduced by 15 per cent. Unemployment benefit dropped 10 per cent, whilst contributions were raised. The benefit period was reduced to 26 weeks in a year and for certain forms of benefit a 'needs' test was applied.

Despite all this, there was a boom in the building of private dwellings for more prosperous wage earners and the lower ranks of clerical workers able to borrow from building societies. A three-bedroomed house in the South of England cost about £500, or £25 down and monthly payments of £4 or £5 per month over 25 years. Elsewhere the price of the same house ranged from £350 to £400. Council house rents cost from seven to 15 shillings a week.

Electricity replaced gas as a form of lighting and electrical goods were sold energetically. Door-to-door salesmen tried to persuade housewives to take on hire-purchase agreements to buy vacuum cleaners. Walls ice-cream men sold 'two-penny bricks' from tricycles bearing the slogan 'Stop Me and Buy One'. Women at work in the cities were symbolized by the Lyons' teashop waitress.

In Germany, Hitler rose to power, while in Britain pacifist trends were the fashion — invoked by the horrors of the First World War and a feeling that it should never happen again.

Neville Chamberlain succeeded Stanley Baldwin as Prime Minister in 1937. He was certain that all disputes could be settled peacefully. This typified the British people's thinking as they craved for knowledge about contemporary social questions and means of righting the world's wrongs. Thus was created an indifference to the situation that was developing in Europe. People, on the whole, were unaware that war was about to break out in 1939.

The decade ended with unemployment falling to near the one million mark. Many jobs were created by the rearmaments programme.

WHO DID WHAT?

NAME THE PERSON OR PERSONS INVOLVED IN THE FOLLOWING EVENTS

Who defeated Republican President Herbert Hoover to become President of the USA in November 1932?

Franklin D. Roosevelt

This was the first of four terms of office (1932, 1936, 1940 and 1944). Roosevelt became a State Senator at 28 and was the Democrat nomination for Vice-President at 38. A year later he contracted poliomyelitis. He triumphed over this and became President 10 years later.

Roosevelt convinced the nation that he would deal with the Depression with plans to boost spending on railways, roads, electric power and farming. He also promised to regulate the banks and the stock market. He said: "No American will starve." He wanted unemployment insurance for all.

Who founded the British Union of Fascists?

Sir Oswald Ernald Mosley

He became MP for Harrow as a Conservative (1918–22), as an Independent (1922–24) and as a Labour MP (1924–30). He was a member of Ramsey MacDonald's government. He formed the British Union of Fascists in 1931. They failed to win any seats in the election that year.

Mosley was a convincing speaker who aroused enthusiasm for his party and caused mob riots during the thirties. He was arrested under the Defence Regulations in 1940 and was interned with a number of his followers.

Whose book, The Shape of Things to Come, *was published in 1933?*

H.G. Wells

The Shape of Things to Come depicted the history of civilization following a global holocaust, after which civilization became a science-based world. Later, it was made into a spectacular film.

H.G. Wells published some 156 works. He tended to follow Utopian ideas, revealing himself to be a reformer far in advance of his age. Earlier novels included *The Time Machine* (1895), *The Invisible Man* (1897) and *The War of the Worlds* (1898).

PUZZLE 1 *WHO DID WHAT?*

With which country did the Vatican sign a pact in July 1933?

Germany
The pact was signed by Cardinal Pacelli, the Papal Secretary of State and Herr von Papen, the German Vice-Chancellor. Within an hour of the signing, Hitler revoked his orders to dissolve all Roman Catholic organizations. Later, in a speech to storm-troopers, he said that the treaty and the disappearance of the Catholic party brought to an end the fight for political power.

Which infamous American gangster blasted his way out of a police trap with a machine gun in St Paul, Minnesota, in March 1934?

John Dillinger
Dillinger was wanted in a number of states for bank robbery and 16 murders. This was the third time he had escaped imprisonment. He was 5' 7" tall, weighed about 153 pounds and claimed to drink little. He had a scar on the back of his left hand and a mole between his eyebrows.

He was shot dead on 22 July 1934 outside a Chicago cinema. He had been watching a Clark Gable gangster film.

Which two new dancing stars sparkled in The Gay Divorcee *(1934)*?

Fred Astaire and Ginger Rogers
These two, for many, became the greatest partnership in the history of the Hollywood musical. The films were escape fantasies for the masses who were struggling with the realities of unemployment and poverty. They included *Top Hat* (1935), *Swing Time* (1936), *Shall We Dance?* (1937) and *Carefree* (1938).

WHO DID WHAT? PUZZLE 1

Which singing star from Rochdale, Lancashire, landed a record film contract to make three films for the sum of £150,000?

Gracie Fields

It was a two-year contract signed in 1935 with Associated Talking Pictures. Gracie was reported to have said: "I don't really like it. There's too much responsibility. Give me a cottage and ten shillings."

She became famous for songs like *Sally* and *The Biggest Aspidistra in the World.* Her real name was Gracie Stansfield

What was the extraordinary exploit of the British aviator, Beryl Markham, in September 1936?

She flew across the Atlantic alone

She was the first woman to do so. Some 5,000 people turned out in New York to greet her. The 33-year-old woman had crash-landed her aircraft on Cape Breton Island, Nova Scotia. She was then flown south to New York. The only sign of the accident was a sticking plaster over one eye.

Which member of the Royal Family said: "I want you to understand that in making up my mind I did not forget the country or the Empire which as Prince of Wales, and lately as King, I have for 25 years tried to serve."?

Edward VIII during his abdication speech

Edward VIII abdicated to marry Wallis Simpson, who had divorced her second husband. She was not considered a suitable person to be Queen. His abdication speech was broadcast on the radio on 11 December 1936. Early the next morning he boarded a destroyer at Portsmouth and left for France to be with Mrs Simpson.

PUZZLE 1 *WHO DID WHAT?*

Which actor caused people to flee into the streets in panic when he broadcast H.G. Well's The War of the Worlds *on American radio in 1938?*

Orson Welles

During the dramatization the 23-year-old actor announced: "Ladies and gentlemen, I have a grave announcement to make. Incredible as it may seem, strange beings who landed in New Jersey to-night are the vanguard of an invading army from Mars."

Thousands of people thought it was real and panicked. Police switchboards were jammed. Some people reported seeing the Martians.

Merle Oberon and Laurence Olivier starred in which classic film, adapted from a book by Emily Brontë and released in 1939?

Wuthering Heights

Heathcliff (Olivier) is a disruptive influence on the lonely, moorland home of the Earnshaws, who had taken him in and raised him. Catherine Earnshaw (Oberon) forms a passionate attachment to Heathcliff, but her brother hates him. After hearing a chance remark from Catherine that it would degrade her to marry him, Heathcliff disappears for three years. When he returns, wealthy and polished, Catherine has married Edgar Linton. Heathcliff then sleeps with Edgar's sister to avenge himself on Catherine.

The adjective 'wuthering' in the title is a Yorkshire word referring to turbulent weather.

Who said in parliament on 3 September 1939: "This country is now at war with Germany. We are ready."?

Neville Chamberlain

Britain had given an ultimatum to Germany at 9am to suspend its attack on Poland. No reply was received. At 11am Chamberlain declared war. Half-an-hour later, an air-raid siren sounded in London, but it was a false alarm. An unidentified aircraft, friendly, had been seen approaching the south coast.

The great newspaper war

To boost circulation and obtain extra advertising revenue, newspapers offered free insurance to readers. A registered reader could get as much as £250,000 for bereaved heirs. This stopped in 1932 and a war with free gifts started. Registered readers received silk stockings, household goods, encyclopaedias and so on.

Each new reader cost the *Daily Herald* £1 and the *Daily Express* 8s 3d. Many readers registered with one paper for a month, then switched to another for more free gifts. In 1933, the race to gain higher circulation was called off. By this time the circulation of both the *Daily Herald* and *Daily Express* had gone up to more than two million.

Grand Hotel (1932)

This black-and-white film starred Greta Garbo, Joan Crawford, John Barrymore, Lionel Barrymore and Wallace Beery, all of whom, it was said, tried to outdo each other.

The story depicts the dramatically intertwined lives of various guests in a Berlin hotel. When all the other characters have been introduced, Greta Garbo, who plays a ballerina, rises swan-like from a tumble of bedclothes. Later in the film she utters the immortal words, "I want to be alone." In fact, she says it three times.

The film won an Academy Award for the best picture of 1932.

Sir Malcolm Campbell

In September 1935, Malcolm Campbell, in his famous car Bluebird, set a new world record of 301.337 mph along the Bonneville Salt Flats in Utah, USA. This broke his own record of 276.816 mph of the previous March.

In August 1939, on Coniston Water in the Lake District, he set the world water speed record by reaching 141.7 mph in his boat, also named Bluebird. This record stood until 1950. He was knighted in 1931.

His son, Donald, whose boats and cars were also named Bluebird, later broke both speed records. Donald died when his boat disintegrated in an attempt to attain a water speed record of 300 mph in 1967.

PUZZLE 2 SCRAMBLE

CAN YOU LINK THE PERSON NAMED WITH THE BOOK, FILM, MUSIC, SPORT OR SUBJECT?

Sir Thomas Beecham	Tennis
Charlie Chaplin	Cakes and Ale
Glen Miller	The Big Sleep
W. Somerset Maugham	Cricket
Shirley Temple	'In the Mood'
John Steinbeck	Tarzan of the Apes
Joe Louis	City Lights
Donald Bradman	The London Philharmonic Orchestra
Raymond Chandler	The Grapes of Wrath
Gary Cooper	Boxing
Johnny Weissmuller	The Little Princess
Fred Perry	A Farewell to Arms

Sir Thomas Beecham

The London Philharmonic Orchestra

Sir Thomas Beecham created both the London Philharmonic (1932) and the Royal Philharmonic (1947) as well as other orchestras. He was the grandson of the founder of the pill-manufacturing firm of the same name. He was particularly associated with the works of Haydn, Mozart and Delius. In 1911, he introduced the Russian ballet to England. He died in 1961, leaving a large legacy of recorded music.

Charlie Chaplin

City Lights (1931)

Charlie Chaplin had a slum childhood. His boyhood home was in Kennington, South London. He had a music hall training. After going to Hollywood in 1914, he became famous, identified by his little bowler hat, smudge moustache, slack trousers and long-toed boots, his flat-footed gait and impassivity. His genius lay in the creation of a universally recognized tragi-comic figure.

Another film, *Modern Times,* was released in 1936.

Glen Miller

'In the Mood' (1939)

Glen Miller was the most influential of all in the popular band field of music and has been imitated by many. He drilled his band to produce the sound he wanted, which was created by a clarinet playing one octave above four saxophones, balanced by trombones and trumpets. He became the world's most popular dance band leader. Other tunes he composed were *Moonlight Serenade* and *Kalamazoo.*

On 16 December 1944, a plane carrying him from England to France vanished without trace. Many fans refused to believe he was dead.

PUZZLE 2 SCRAMBLE

W. Somerset Maugham

Cakes and Ale (1930)

Maugham was a novelist, short-story writer and playwright. His work was distinguished by skilful craftsmanship, satire, cynicism and ironical detachment. He used his own experiences as background for his stories. *Cakes and Ale* was about a famous novelist. *Ashenden* (1928) was based on his experience as a First World War secret agent. His medical background was used for his first novel, *Liza of Lambeth* (1897) and *Of Human Bondage* (1915). He was also a great traveller and set many of his stories in the tropics.

Shirley Temple

The Little Princess (1939)

Temple was the biggest box-office draw of the thirties. Her other films included: *The Red-Haired Alibi* (1932), *The Littlest Rebel* (1935) and *Dimples* (1936). Louis B. Mayer tried unsuccessfully to steal her from MGM to play Dorothy in *The Wizard of Oz* (1939). Although she made a number of later films, her popularity faded when she grew up. As Shirley Temple-Black she took an interest in politics and became a US Ambassador to the United Nations.

John Steinbeck

The Grapes of Wrath (1939)

Steinbeck studied marine biology but left university before he got a degree. He worked as a labourer, caretaker and fruit-picker before becoming known as a writer. His novels reflect life in the Depression. *The Grapes of Wrath* depicts the story of a family of sharecroppers dispossessed in Oklahoma and who travel west to land promised them in California. Other books include *Of Mice and Men* (1937) and *East of Eden* (1952). He won the Nobel Prize for Literature in 1962.

Joe Louis

Boxing

Popularly known as the 'Brown Bomber from Detroit' because of his destructive fists, Louis won the world heavyweight championship in 1937 by knocking out Jimmy Braddock in the eighth round. Braddock, who had been champion two years running, was so badly hurt he had to be carried from the ring. Louis held the title, defending it 25 times, until 1948, when he retired undefeated. In 1950, he made a comeback but was outpointed by Ezzard Charles.

Donald Bradman

Cricket

He was born in Australia in 1908 and became the most successful batsman of his time. In his first test in England at Trent Bridge (1930) he made 131, then 254 at Lords, 334 at Leeds and 232 at the Oval. A small man who frequently wore the baggy green cap of Australia, Bradman earned himself a reputation as a batting machine without a soul — he scored 29 Test centuries. He did not like being second and was said to have changed cricket into a game which was no longer merely a game to be enjoyed and savoured.

Raymond Chandler

The Big Sleep **(1939)**

Chandler began writing detective fiction for magazines. *The Big Sleep* was his first novel. His most famous character is the private eye Philip Marlowe, who is tough, laconically wise-cracking, a man of honour and hard up. His clients are usually rich and corrupt. The stories are mostly set in the Los Angeles of the thirties and forties.

Chandler's books have been highly praised as works of art, despite their sometimes over-lush language.

PUZZLE 2 SCRAMBLE

Gary Cooper

A Farewell to Arms (1932)

Cooper plays an American lieutenant in the Italian ambulance service who falls in love with an English nurse during the First World War. The film was adapted from Ernest Hemingway's book of the same title. Cooper represents — in most of his films — the slow-talking, slow to anger, on-the-level, honest American good guy.

Johnny Weissmuller

Tarzan of the Apes (1932)

Johnny Weissmuller was the first man to swim 100 metres in under a minute (1922). He dominated the 1924 Olympics and also took part in the 1928 games, winning his fifth gold medal. He set 24 world records, some of which stood for over 10 years. He modelled swimwear for advertisements, resulting in his being noticed by MGM studios. Thus began his career as the first and the best-loved Tarzan on the screen.

Fred Perry

Tennis

Fred Perry was one of the most successful tennis players of the thirties. He won the Wimbledon singles in 1934, 1935 and 1936 — the first time such a feat had been done since 1912. He also played table tennis and was winner of the World Table Tennis Championship in 1929.

Hire-purchase

Hire-purchase was an innovation of the 1930s, which enabled people with capital to buy 10 times more households goods than before. But it was still not seen as quite respectable: leading hire-purchase firms guaranteed to deliver their furniture in plain vans.

Fashions

In 1930, 'beach pyjamas' with wide, flapping trousers became the rage. They remained in fashion for several years. Skirts and hair tended to be worn long. Soft waved hairstyles were popular — the permanent wave was well established. Out-of-doors, shorts had begun to be worn and slacks were becoming acceptable casual wear for women.

In the early thirties, healthy exposure to sun and sea was becoming a recognized weekend tonic. The increasing number of sun-worshippers led to special 'sun suits' made up of brassière top, shorts and coatee in gay patterns. By 1935, the two-piece in wool had become popular.

Towards the end of the decade, skirts became shorter and hairstyles such as the page-boy bob were fashionable. Smart pill-box hats were worn with an elastic band under the hair at the back. There was also a trend of wearing almost crownless hats tipped over one eye. About 1937, the 'snood' — a caul or veil of heavy net — became fashionable. Many women went hatless but carried a scarf for emergencies.

For men, over-the-head shirts continued until about 1935. By then, American coat-style shirts, put on like a coat and buttoned up, were becoming popular.

Oil lamps

60 per cent of rural homes still used oil lamps in 1939, at which time most people in towns had electricity. It was also offered on new council estates and in new private dwellings.

What did Mahatma Gandhi do between 12 March and 6 April 1930, because of British law and salt?

A 300-mile protest march

He walked from his home near Jalalpur to the Golf of Cambay to protest against and defy British law which had established a government monopoly on producing salt. His intention was to take a symbolic amount of salt from the sea water and allow himself to be arrested. He was thwarted by the police, who had stirred the salt deposits into mud.

Later, in May, he was arrested in a clampdown which attempted to deal with his disobedience. This sparked riots, strikes and the burning of property throughout India.

What happened to the French President, Paul Doumer, in May 1932 at the Rothschild Foundation building?

He was assassinated

President Doumer was attending a charity event where books were being sold for the benefit of ex-servicemen authors. As he talked to one of the authors, a man pushed forward holding a gun, fired and shouted: "This is only the beginning!"

The President died 14 hours later in hospital. The assassin was a White Russian émigré who hated Communism. Doctors pronounced him insane.

What happened to the German Reichstag in Berlin on 27 February 1933?

It went up in flames

When firemen arrived, the building was burning in several places. A young Dutchman, described as a simple-minded Communist hanger-on, was arrested. Hermann Goering, on arrival at the scene, said: "This is a Communist crime against the new government. We will show no mercy. Every Communist must be shot on the spot."

The destruction of the building enabled Adolf Hitler to prevail on the ageing President Von Hindenburg to sign a decree suspending all legal guarantees for personal liberty, freedom of speech and the Press and any right of assembly. He had, at last, got the dictatorial powers he wanted.

The gutted, smoke-blackened building was said to represent the funeral pyre of democracy.

What happened on 23 May 1934 in Louisiana, to Clyde Barrow and Bonnie Parker?

They were shot in an ambush by Texas Rangers

Over a four-year period, Bonnie and Clyde had robbed banks, power stations and diners. In the process they had killed at least 12 people. They were only in their mid-twenties when they drove into the ambush and died.

What celebration took place in London on 6 May 1935, involving King George V and Queen Mary?

Silver Jubilee

The King wore the scarlet uniform of a Field Marshal and Queen Mary wore white to celebrate their 25 years as monarchs. Both Princess Elizabeth and her younger sister, Princess Margaret Rose, were present in St Paul's Cathedral.

However, the scene-stealer of the day was a mongrel dog who trotted in front of the royal carriage and then hid underneath it. Soldiers and police failed in their attempts to catch him. He became known as the 'Jubilee Dog'.

What took place in the Royal Tombs at Windsor in January 1936?

King George V was laid to rest

King George V became the best known monarch in history, owing to the radio, which had become popular. In 1932, he started the broadcasting of messages to families on Christmas day afternoons. His most famous saying was: "I don't like abroad, I've been there." He had five sons and one daughter.

PUZZLE 3 *WHAT HAPPENED?*

What happened in Southampton docks on 27 May 1936, concerning the Queen Mary?

She left on her maiden voyage to America

The *Queen Mary* left Southampton for Cherbourg and New York — about 3,000 miles — with 1,840 passengers on board. Crowds cheered, a band played and small boats filled with spectators escorted her away from the docks. A goodwill message was sent to the commander by the king (Edward VIII). During the voyage regular broadcasts were made about life on board.

The price of a transatlantic trip on board the ship had been advertised as being from £37 5s, which included meals and hotels. In August 1936, the *Queen Mary* crossed the Atlantic in record time — 3 days, 23 hours and 57 minutes.

Which world sporting event took place in Berlin in August 1936?

The Olympic Games

The Games had been awarded to Berlin before Hitler came to power. Moves to organize a boycott failed when the Germans put forward a few token Jewish competitors to counteract criticism.

The star of the games, and a source of great embarrassment to Hitler, was the black athlete Jessie Owens. He won the 100 and 200 metres, the long jump and led his team to victory in the 400 metre relay. Hitler left the sports stadium to avoid shaking hands with him.

What happened at Crystal Palace on 29 November 1936?

It caught fire

Thousands of people gathered to watch the flames while about 500 firemen fought the blaze. Sightseers turned out from as far away as Margate and Brighton. Special trains were laid on from London stations and the queues of traffic held up fire engines trying to get to the scene. The pilot of an airliner reported that he could see the blaze from mid-Channel and a warning was given to routine flights to avoid chartered planes flying over the scene.

WHAT HAPPENED? PUZZLE 3

What happened at Westminster Abbey on 12 May 1937, involving King George VI and Queen Elizabeth?

Their coronation

George VI succeeded his brother Edward VIII, who had abdicated to marry Mrs Simpson. George VI struggled against ill health, natural shyness and a reserved manner to earn respect and love throughout the Commonwealth. He had two daughters, Princess Elizabeth Alexandra Mary, Duchess of Edinburgh, who succeeded him as sovereign, and Princess Margaret Rose.

What happened in Poland on 1 September 1939?

Poland was invaded by German forces

The swift attack gave the English language a new word, 'blitzkrieg', meaning lightning war. The Polish defences, based on trench warfare, were no match for the fast-moving armoured forces which were combined with air-strikes. In eight days the German forces covered over 140 miles and reached the gates of Warsaw, which was then devastated by two weeks of nightmarish bombing.

On 17 September, Russia also invaded and on 28 September the partition of Poland was agreed. This divided up Poland, giving the eastern region to Russia and the west to Germany. The Polish government fled to Romania and the state of Poland ceased to exist.

What happened in June 1939 in Liverpool Bay, involving the new submarine, Thetis?

She sank

The submarine sank during trials, with the loss of 70 lives. Her stern was spotted sticking above the water. Messages were tapped on her hull to men inside. Rescue attempts continued for three days. Hawsers were passed underneath the vessel and her bows were hauled to the surface. Six men jumped out before the cables snapped and the submarine sank back beneath the surface.

Going to the cinema

The most popular form of entertainment was going to the 'flicks'. One survey estimated that 40 per cent of the population saw one film a week and 25 per cent saw two. By 1939, attendance had risen to 50 per cent of the population. In 1937, British Gaumont owned 345 cinemas, Associated British Cinemas 431 and Odeon 900. A further 3,000 were privately owned and had names such as Ritz, Majestic, Rialto, Astoria and Granada.

George Orwell wrote in 1937: "You can always get a seat for fourpence and at a matinee at some houses you can even get a seat for twopence. Even people on the verge of starvation will readily pay twopence to get out of the ghastly cold of a winter afternoon."

Most of the films were pure escapism. Working people were only too glad to forget the reality of the Depression for a few hours. The cinema brought relief.

Population fears

Before the thirties the population had been growing at such a rate that experts were sounding the alarm. In 1931, there were just under 40 million people in England and nearly 45 million in Great Britain. For most of the thirties the birth rate fell to under 15 per thousand. Experts were now predicting a steep decline in the population.

Public Information Booklets

The Protection of Your Home Against Air Raids was a 36-page, buff-covered booklet which advised the 'head of the house to consider himself the captain of a ship'. It compared the taking of precautions to lifeboat drill – essential, even if unlikely to be needed. This was followed in July and August 1939 by leaflets on subjects such as 'Your Gas Mask' and 'Masking Your Windows'. There was also a 48-page booklet entitled *The National Service Handbook*. This was described by the Prime Minister, in January 1939, as 'A scheme to make us ready for war'.

The introduction of the short skirt as a fashion resulted in the loss of the sale of more than two hundred million yards of cotton cloth a year.

True

After short skirts became fashionable, the sale of petticoats dropped drastically. One industry boss commented: "Where our daughters wear three or four yards of cotton cloth, our mothers used to wear ten."

In May 1930, the industry held a National Cotton Week. More than 10,000 shops around the country tried to increase sales for an ailing industry. Women, it was said, were being tempted to spend money on other kinds of goods rather than fabrics, as had been their grandmothers' custom.

The number of people unemployed broke the two million barrier in August 1930.

True

The figure for people unemployed was 2,011,467. Of these 1,431,505 were men, 56,024 boys, 476,041 women and 47,897 girls. It was the highest total since 1921. The figure rose to nearly three million in 1933 and remained above two million for most of the decade. There were many protest marches and men moved from the areas where industry — cotton, mining, shipbuilding — was declining, to seek employment with the newer car and electrical goods manufacturers.

The 1932 Olympic Games were held in New York.

False

They were held in Los Angeles. There were fears that attendance would be poor. However, athletes' travel was subsidized, an Olympic village was built and the Coliseum turned out to be a big attraction for crowds.

Tommy Hampson won four gold medals for Britain. Mildred 'Babe' Didrikson — an 18-year-old American typist — gave the most remarkable performance by setting a world record for the 80 metres hurdles, winning gold in the javelin and a silver medal in the high jump. She expressed disgust at only being allowed to enter three events.

PUZZLE 4 *TRUE OR FALSE?*

'Dietrickery' was a fashion trend for women to wear men's clothes and was started by Marlene Dietrich.

True

Grey flannel trousers were particularly popular. The actress caused a sensation in Paris, where there was a law against women attracting 'undue attention' by walking the streets dressed in male clothing. She arrived from America dressed in a man's brown suit, coat and beret. She was mobbed by the crowds.

It was officially confirmed, in August 1933, that the Nazis had begun rounding up large numbers of Jews and sending them to concentration camps.

True

A committee of German experts had been formed to consider measures to increase the size of German families and recommend ways of putting an end to the 'mixture of races and degeneration of German families'.

Victims were arrested on charges of 'fighting storm-troopers' or 'consorting with German girls'. The outlawed Socialist Party claimed that 45,000 prisoners were being held in 65 camps, the largest being Dachau. Not all of the prisoners were Jews. Anyone attempting to escape was shot without challenge.

In 1934, a slimming craze was blamed for a dramatic slump in the British potato market.

True

The slimmer look became the rage because of the fashion — short skirts, bobbed hair and a boyish look. The Potato Marketing Board launched a campaign 'to convince the fair sex that they are on the wrong lines when they cut out potatoes to get slim'. The trend met criticism, mostly by men who fancied women who were more curvy, and doctors who said that women were putting their health at risk.

TRUE OR FALSE? PUZZLE 4

Winston Churchill advocated the cutting of spending on defence in November 1934. He said that Germany would not dare attack Britain.

False

He advised strongly that the government should spend more on defence. He warned the House of Commons that German munition factories were working 'under practically war conditions' and that by 1937 Germany's airforce would be twice the size of Britain's. He said that, while there was no reason to think that Germany would attack, it was not pleasant to feel that she could.

In 1936, Salvador Dali, the surrealist painter, gave an international lecture in London wearing a diving suit.

True

The lecture could not be heard through the helmet. What he was saying was: "Let me out!" but no one could hear him. The helmet had stuck, resulting in his nearly suffocating.

Dali was a Spanish painter and sculptor. His paintings depicted nightmares and hallucinations, and often included figures drawn with extreme realism. He also made films, wrote books and designed ballets.

In 1937, George Orwell's book, The Road to Brighton Pier, *was published.*

False

It was entitled *The Road to Wigan Pier* and provides a picture and discussion of social problems of the time. Orwell, in his lifetime, was often thought of as being politically to the left but he was, in fact, distrustful of all political parties. His other books of the period include *Down and Out in Paris and London* (1933) and *Homage to Catalonia* (1938).

PUZZLE 4 _TRUE OR FALSE?_

Half the city of Cardiff was sold for 20 million pounds in 1938.

True

It was the largest property deal to that date in British history. The deal comprised about 20,000 houses, 1,000 shops and 250 public houses, and included theatres, farmland and villages. All this property belonged to the estate of the Marquis of Bute. He was descended from Robert III, who was King of Scotland in the fourteenth century. Lord Bute was said to have joined the army in the First World War as a private on a wage of 2s 9d a day, under the family name of Crichton-Smith.

Air-raid shelters were provided free to all households.

False

To qualify for a free shelter, families had to be earning less than £250 a year. Priority was given to London and other target cities which were likely to be bombed.

The shelters were tunnel-shaped, made of steel and could be erected by two people without experience. They measured 6' 6" by 4' 6" and needed to be partly sunk into the ground. They could be extended to accommodate large families.

The battleship Graf Spee, _the pride of the German Fleet, was scuttled by her crew in December 1939._

True

Three British cruisers, _Exeter_, _Ajax_ and _Achilles_, tracked down the _Graf Spee_, attacked her and forced her to limp into Montevideo harbour. The Uruguayan government threatened to intern the ship if she did not put back to sea. Hitler himself ordered that she should be scuttled. Her captain, Hans Lansdorf, shot himself in the head and her crew blew her up. Thousands who watched, expecting the battleship to return to the battle, saw instead the huge explosion as she blew up.

Amy Johnson

The attitude that women were mere domestic ornaments had begun to change. Women, like Amy Johnson, began to make contributions to national affairs. Amy, a 25-year-old secretary from Hull, surprised everyone in May 1930 by flying solo from Croydon to Australia in 20 days. She had obtained her pilot's licence only 10 months before and flew a second-hand Gypsy Moth she had bought for £600. She was the first lone woman pilot.

During the flight she coped with numerous mishaps which included a broken airscrew — she carried a spare strapped to the fuselage. Also, sand storms forced her to land in Java.

In 1936, she made another record-breaking flight to the Cape and back, beating both outward and homeward records.

During the Second World War she flew aircraft from factories to airfields. In 1941, she ran out of fuel over the Thames Estuary, parachuted out of her aircraft and was drowned. She was 38.

Amy Johnson was a romantic figure of the thirties. Songsters hailed her as 'Wonderful Amy, the Aeroplane Girl'.

The Means Test

As dole queues lengthened in 1933, benefits were cut. A man was entitled to benefit under the employment insurance scheme only if he had paid 30 contributions in two years and then the entitlement lasted for just six months. Dole then became subject to the 'new' test. Its aim was to cut local authority spending. The amount of money given was supposed to relate to household needs.

Officials visited homes and checked up on savings and expenditure. A child earning a few pence on a paper round would have his earnings deducted from the amount allowed. An old age pensioner or a widower living with one of their children were counted as lodgers and this resulted in deductions being made.

In 1934, relief became 'assistance' rather than dole. Men sat at home or in working men's clubs, rarely able to afford a drink. Very few could afford holidays. One man who worked in a shipyard said he had worked for one year out of 12. He and his family — a wife and five children — lived on unemployment pay of £1 13s. Their diet was mainly bread, margarine and tea.

CAN YOU PUZZLE OUT THE CONNECTION BETWEEN THE FOLLOWING?

Uruguay
Football
30 July 1930

The First World Cup Tournament

The tournament was not thought by all nations to be a genuine world competition. The British football association was not invited to participate. Four other nations — Italy, Holland, Spain and Sweden — who had also bid to hold the competition stayed away, as did Hungary, Austria and Germany.

Uruguay, the smallest nation, recovered from being 2–1 down at half-time to beat Argentina 4–2 in the final.

An experimental laboratory
Menloo Park, New Jersey
Inventions
The electric light bulb

Thomas Edison

Thomas Edison started work as a newsboy and later trained as a telegraph operator. This led him to invent and patent many improvements to telegraphic equipment. With the money he made from these he set up a laboratory in Menloo Park, making inventions in many fields.

One of the problems he solved was producing moving pictures on a screen. He was the most prolific of inventors and had over 1,300 patents to his credit when he died at his home in New Jersey on 18 October 1931. He was 84.

The Nobel Prize for Literature, 1932
The Forsyte Saga
The pseudonym, John Sinjohn
Combe, Surrey

John Galsworthy

He was born in Combe, Surrey in 1867. He studied law but he only practised briefly. His first four novels were published under the pseudonym of John Sinjohn. As well as writing novels, which included *The Forsyte Saga*, he was a very successful playwright. Some 31 full-length plays were produced in London, as well as a number of one-acts. He first became popular with the success of *The Man of Property* (1906) and his play, *The Silver Box* (1906).

Fay Wray
An outsized ape
Films

King Kong (1933)

In this fantasy film the central character, a giant gorilla, falls in love with the heroine played by Fay Wray. King Kong was very important to later science fiction pictures. The special effects used to animate the gorilla and his fellow monsters paved the way for future, more controlled special effects.

September 1934
Gresford, Near Wrexham
262 dead

A pit disaster

It was the first pit disaster for 21 years. One miner inched his way to safety up a 200 foot vertical shaft which was two feet wide. Outbreaks of fire hampered rescue work, causing intense heat and fumes. Men could work for only three minutes before collapsing.

Paperback books
Sixpence
Allen Lane

Penguin paperbacks

The publishers, Allen Lane, launched a new type of book with paper covers in 1935. They were coloured white and orange and had a drawing of a penguin on them.

The notion of paperbacks had originated in America. Lane's idea was to produce his paperbacks as quality books. His declared intention was 'to publish in a form and at a price which the ordinary people could afford to buy all the great books of our culture'.

There was initial resistance by the book trade but, by 1950, Penguins had become an 'institution' in Britain.

*The people's car
Ferdinand Porsche
An air-cooled engine, mounted at
the rear*

The Volkswagen

In February 1936, Adolf Hitler opened the first factory for the manufacture of Germany's 'people's car'. It was intended for mass-production at low prices. The car was supposed to do for Germany what Henry Ford had done for the United States.

*Idealists
Spain
General Franco
July 1936*

The Spanish Civil War

In July 1936, General Franco led a rising of the Foreign Legion in Morocco to overthrow the newly elected government formed by Socialists, Communists, Anarchists and Liberals, known as the 'Popular Front'.

Idealists from all over the world went to Spain to fight in the Civil War. Some, opposed to Fascism, joined the Popular Front side. Others, often from the same towns and schools, fought for General Franco's Nationalists, convinced that they must stop the spread of Communism.

Many intellectuals joined in this war. One such notable was George Orwell, who joined the International Brigade to fight against General Franco. Many of them, totally unprepared for war, died. An estimated 59,000 foreign volunteers fought in the war.

*An air journey from Frankfurt
to New Jersey
Static electricity
Hydrogen gas
An explosion on 6 May 1937*

The airship Hindenburg

As the giant airship prepared to moor in New Jersey she exploded in a ball of fire. There had been a thunderstorm and the airship had waited for a lull in it to land. It was thought that the accident may have been caused by static electricity igniting the airship's hydrogen gas. Some 33 passengers and crew died. The £380,000 airship had previously made 10 safe trips across the Atlantic.

A chateau in a valley near Tours
Wallis Simpson
A ceremony
3 June 1937

The Duke of Windsor married Wallis Simpson

The ceremony was simple, with only a few witnesses, although hundreds of French sightseers arrived to watch the event. The first ceremony, conducted by the mayor of Monts, complied with French civil law. A few minutes later the couple were married under the rites of the Church of England by the Vicar of St Bride's, Doncaster. Later, after a buffet, they left to honeymoon in Austria.

A steam-engine called 'Mallard'
Newcastle and London
126mph
3 July 1938

The world record speed for steam-engines

'Mallard', a Gresley A4 Pacific steam-engine on a track between Newcastle and London, proved itself to be the fastest locomotive in the world. It achieved a speed of 126mph for 300 yards on a stretch of track near Peterborough and maintained a speed of 120mph for more than five miles. This beat the record of 114mph set by 'Coronation Scot' on the Euston line the previous year. Nigel Gresley, the engine's designer, was on board at the time.

A scarecrow
A tin man
A cowardly lion
Judy Garland

The Wizard of Oz (1939)

The film made a star of 17-year-old Judy Garland, who played Dorothy, the central character. A scarecrow (Ray Bolger), a tin man (Jack Haley) and a cowardly lion (Bert Lahr) go off with Dorothy to find the Wizard of Oz. One of the best remembered songs from the film, which became strongly identified with Judy Garland, was Harold Arlen's 'Over the Rainbow'

Going to school

Children were taught under conditions which had existed for 40 years. The traditional, church-style buildings were often antiquated, badly ventilated and overcrowded. Many schools still used earth closets. In 1935, there were still 6,000 classes with over 50 pupils in England and Wales and 56 with over 60 children. By 1939, this had been reduced to 2,000 classes with over 50 pupils.

Talk and chalk

Teaching methods were formal. The alphabet, mathematical tables and chunks of nineteenth-century history were learnt by heart and chanted by the class. Teachers drummed facts into pupils' heads by repeating them many times and writing them on the blackboard. This method became known as 'talk and chalk'. There was little participation or discussion and barely any attention was given to individuals. Music meant singing in chorus, usually hymns or patriotic songs. Discipline was always given top priority.

Evacuation

At the end of the decade, in preparation for possible bombing, children were voluntarily evacuated from 40 highly populated areas. Over a few days, three-quarters of a million school children and many thousand under-age children were moved to rural areas.

Parents were not given any guarantee where their children would go. Many East End children with a poor standard of cleanliness were housed with families who were fastidious. This opened the eyes of the public to the conditions that so many children lived in.

However, the expected bombing in the winter of 1939 never happened. Thousands of children left their billets and returned home. This created problems, as their previous schools could not be used until air-raid shelters had been provided. During this period, nine months of education was lost.

Under the Spreading Chestnut Tree

A popular rhyme was sung by children in playgrounds to this tune:

> Under the spreading chestnut tree,
> Neville Chamberlain said to me:
> If you want to get your gas mask free,
> Join the blinking ARP!

The rhyme was, in fact, misleading. Gas masks were free whether you joined the ARP (air-raid precautions) or not, although a better type of mask was given to ARP workers.

FAMOUS PEOPLE CROSSWORD PUZZLE 6

DRAW THIS CROSSWORD ON A BLACKBOARD, PHOTOCOPY THIS PAGE AND GIVE IT TO EACH PERSON, OR USE THE CLUES AS A STRAIGHT QUIZ

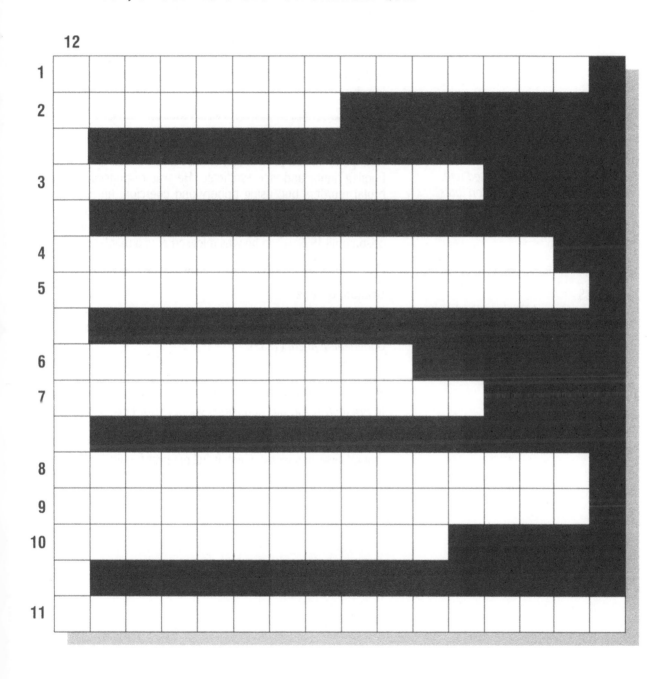

1 ACROSS
She played a cabaret singer in the film, The Blue Angel, *in 1930.*

Marlene Dietrich

The Blue Angel was her first big hit. She also starred in *Morocco* (1930) with Gary Cooper, *Shanghai Express* (1932) and *Destry Rides Again* (1939). She usually played the vamp, the mistress for whom men ruined themselves. Later, in the fifties, she developed an international cabaret career which brought more fans, fame and a cult following. Her real name was Maria Magdalena von Losch.

2 ACROSS
A notorious American gangster known as 'Scarface', who was charged with offences against the prohibition laws in 1931.

Al Capone

Al Capone settled in Chicago in 1920 and became the head of a bootleg liquor and vice syndicate. He was responsible for many brutal murders but, using bribery and coercion, he managed to avoid being tried for them. In 1931, he was finally brought to trial, for tax evasion dating back to 1922, and convicted. He remained in prison until 1939, when he was released after a mental collapse.

3 ACROSS
He wrote the novel, Brighton Rock *(1938).*

Graham Greene

His other books which were published in the thirties include: *Rumour at Nightfall* (1931), *A Gun for Sale* (1936) and *The Confidential Agent* (1939).

Green divided his output between serious novels and what he called 'entertainments'. Most of his novels involve criminal activity. His sympathy always seems to lie with the sinful and their suffering. In *Brighton Rock*, the abnoxious young hero, Pinkie, is presented as being capable of goodness. The novel is set in the dingy under-world of the seaside resort. Pinkie, because of his Catholic back-ground, lives in a world which is full of terror for him.

FAMOUS PEOPLE CROSSWORD PUZZLE 6

4 ACROSS
He composed the opera, Arabella *(1933).*

Richard Strauss

He was a German composer and conductor, born in Munich in 1864. His other works include *Don Quixote* (1897), *Der Rosenkavalier* (1911) and *Daphne* (1938). His last opera was *Capriccio* (1942). He composed some of the greatest German operas. For invention and sheer technical skill, he had few equals in his period.

5 ACROSS
He wrote the novels, Death in the Afternoon *(1932) and* To Have and Have Not *(1937).*

Ernest Hemingway

Death in the Afternoon is a study of bullfighting and *To Have and Have Not* is a short novel about smuggling in the Caribbean.

Hemingway used his own experiences to provide backgrounds for his novels. During the First World War, he served in an American ambulance unit and with the Italian army. Later, he took an active part in the Spanish Civil War. He also lived in Paris and was a war correspondent in France during the Second World War.

Two of his other novels were *A Farewell to Arms* (1929) and *For Whom the Bell Tolls* (1940). He won the Nobel Prize for Literature in 1954.

6 ACROSS
He led the famous 'Long March' (1934–6) and later became head of state in the Chinese Republic.

Mao Tse-tung

Mao Tse-tung led his Chinese rebel Communist forces (80,000 strong) in a 6,000-mile march to avoid defeat by the Nationalist armies. The march took over 12 months and entailed fighting and a great deal of suffering as they made their way through hostile country. Only 20,000 of those who started out reached the safety of their destination, Yenon. Despite the heavy losses, the feat established Mao as the undisputed leader of hard-core Communists and a permanent threat to the Nationalist Government.

PUZZLE 6 *FAMOUS PEOPLE CROSSWORD*

7 ACROSS
He composed the popular songs 'Top Hat' (1935) and 'Cheek to Cheek' (1935).

Irving Berlin
Berlin was an American composer who was born in Russia in 1888. He composed more than 1,000 popular songs, despite the fact that he was unable to read music. He played the notes on his 'Buick' piano and his musical secretary transcribed what he heard. Other songs he wrote which became popular were 'Alexander's Ragtime Band' (1911) and, the best known of them all, 'White Christmas' (1954).

8 ACROSS
He took the part of Quasimodo in the film, The Hunchback of Notre Dame *(1939).*

Charles Laughton
Charles Laughton was probably at his most watchable when he played over-the-top villains. Other films he made in the period were *The Sign of the Cross* (1932), *The Barretts of Wimpole Street* (1934) and *Mutiny on the Bounty* (1935). He was supposedly difficult to direct. Alfred Hitchcock was reported to have said that the best a director could do on a Laughton picture was referee it.

9 ACROSS
An American who won her sixth Wimbledon singles championship in 1933.

Helen Wills Moody
She won the final against the British challenger from Dudley, Dorothy Round, 6–4, 6–8, 6–3. The first two sets were so close that the centre court crowd became almost hysterical. The match reached a pitch when Dorothy Round took the second set after a long and heated argument between two line judges and the umpire. The incident unsettled both women and the American won by making fewer errors.

Helen Wills Moody dominated women's tennis from 1923 to 1938.

FAMOUS PEOPLE CROSSWORD PUZZLE 6

10 ACROSS
He composed 'The Enigma Variations' (1899) and died on 23 February 1934, within sight of the Malvern Hills.

11 ACROSS
The popular name given to the author of The Seven Pillars of Wisdom, *who died on 19 May 1935 after a motor-cycle accident near his cottage, 'Clouds' Hill', in Dorset.*

12 DOWN
Her only novel, Gone with the Wind, *was published in 1936 and won the Pulitzer Prize for fiction in 1937.*

Edward Elgar
Elgar had no formal musical training: apart from some violin lessons, he was self-taught. He succeeded his father as church organist in Worcester and gained early experience as a bandmaster at Worcester County lunatic asylum. Later, he became conductor of the London Symphony Orchestra. After his wife died, in 1920, Elgar practically abandoned composing. His other popular works included the 'Pomp and Circumstance' marches (1901–7).

Lawrence of Arabia
T.E. Lawrence became known as Lawrence of Arabia because of the part he played in organizing Arab resistance behind the Turkish lines during the First World War. He became a legend. This was a problem both to the authorities and to himself. He sought anonymity in the RAF as 'Aircraftsman Ross'. More publicity led him to disappear again, this time using the name 'Shaw'.

The accident occurred when he was on his way home from Bovington army camp. He swerved to avoid hitting two boy cyclists.

Margaret Mitchell
Margaret Mitchell was an American journalist from Georgia. She spent nine years researching and writing her novel. It was to become the classic romance of the American Civil War. The book interweaves the passionate triumphs and tragedies of the heroine, Scarlett O'Hara, with the war and the agony of reconstruction afterwards. The novel is probably the most famous bestseller of the century.

the 1940s

THE FORTIES began with the European powers caught up in a military struggle. The casualties of the Second World War were unprecedented. The total dead was estimated at over 55 million — civilians as well as combatants. The Soviet Union lost some 20 million people. And only a small minority of the Jewish population of Europe remained alive after the war.

Europe faced years of reconstruction and Clement Attlee, Britain's new Prime Minister after victory in the general election on 5 July 1945, warned of post-war austerity measures. World food shortages meant that similar sacrifices to those made during the war years would have to continue. In fact, rationing in 1948 was even more stringent than during the war.

When voting for a Labour government, the electorate were indicating that they wanted equal justice. The traditional deference to the upper classes had been abandoned during the war — exemption from the forces and food rationing had been based on the national need, not on privilege. People wanted this social and economic equality to continue in peacetime.

During this period, industrial depression and unemployment appeared to have been abolished. No one feared being given the sack and people enjoyed lots of overtime. This was said to have removed the incentive for hard work.

Between 1946 and 1949, the Labour government put through a programme of nationalization — the Bank of England (1946), the Coal Industry and Gas (1947), Civil Aviation, Public Transport and Electricity (1948) and Iron and Steel (1949). Vitally important, the National Health Service, set up under the Act of 1946, was to provide — at virtually no cost to the individual — hospital and specialist medical attention. This included general practitioners, dental and ophthalmic services, as well as drugs, medicines, spectacles and dentures.

Many women, recruited to do men's jobs and who had never worked before the war, found that the experience of being self-supporting and independent gave them a feeling of freedom. After the war a large number of them returned to making homes for their families, but a new feeling had been roused — the feminist spirit. Never again would women as a class allow themselves to be regarded as inferior by the all-powerful male.

The forties ended with the superpowers — the United States and the Soviet Union — locked in the entrenched position of a cold war.

WHO DID WHAT?

WHO DID WHAT? PUZZLE 1

NAME THE PERSON OR PERSONS INVOLVED IN THE FOLLOWING EVENTS

Who won an American Academy Award in March 1940 for her performance as Scarlett O'Hara in the film Gone with the Wind?

Vivien Leigh

Vivien Leigh's outstanding beauty was a handicap, as critics had difficulty seeing her acting talents beneath the looks. She was married to Laurence Olivier for many years — again, she may have suffered from being seen as Mrs Olivier. Although she made many other films, including *A Streetcar Named Desire* (1949), she is best remembered for her role as Scarlett O'Hara.

Who was the head of RAF Fighter Command during the Battle of Britain?

Sir Hugh Dowding

He had seen action as a Royal Flying Corps observer and pilot on the Western Front in the First World War. It was due to Sir Hugh Dowding that Fighter Command was better prepared for war than other sections of the British forces. If the Luftwaffe had knocked Fighter Command out before 17 September 1940, it is likely that invasion would have followed. Dowding's 'Battle of Britain' victory saved the country and opened the way for Hitler to be defeated.

Who landed in Scotland with a peace offering from Hitler in May 1941?

Rudolf Hess

Hess was a close friend and confidant of Hitler. He was made deputy leader and heir apparent to Hitler in 1932. In one of the most astounding events of the war, he flew alone to Scotland in a Messerschmitt fighter plane with proposals for a compromise peace with Britain.

He crash-landed near Glasgow and was found with a broken ankle by a ploughman. He said that he had an important message for the Duke of Hamilton.

His proposals were discredited by Germany and rejected by Britain. He was then interned in Britain for the remainder of the war. Later, at Nuremberg (1946), he was found guilty of war crimes and sentenced to life imprisonment.

PUZZLE 1 *WHO DID WHAT?*

Who opened an attack in North Africa against British and Commonwealth troops in March 1941?

General Erwin Rommel

The advance guard of the Afrika Corps landed in Tripoli in February 1941, commanded by General Rommel. His orders from Hitler were to rescue Mussolini's forces, which had suffered humiliating defeats by the British army. In March 1941, he launched his first attack against British and Commonwealth troops. By early 1942, he had driven the Allied forces in the Western Desert back across Libya to El Alamein, inside the Egyptian frontier.

Which army did General Bernard Montgomery lead to triumph at El Alamein in October 1942?

The Eighth Army

General Montgomery was appointed Commander of the Eighth Army in August 1942, and then in October he led them to victory. The Eighth Army pushed Rommel's forces back across Libya to Tripoli. In March 1943, Montgomery again defeated Rommel's army at the battle of the El Mareth line and at Akarit. Montgomery remained with the Eighth Army for the invasion of Sicily and Italy, but then left to prepare for the liberation of France.

Who wrote the screenplay and starred in the classic war film, In Which We Serve *(1942)?*

Noel Coward

The film, written with the help of Lord Louis Mountbatten, depicts the sinking of a destroyer and the emotions of the crew as they struggle to survive. Noel Coward played the captain. The film also starred Bernard Miles, John Mills and Richard Attenborough. Audiences cheered it.

Other films which Coward wrote and produced in the 1940s were *This Happy Breed* (1944), *Blithe Spirit* (1945) and *Brief Encounter* (1946).

WHO DID WHAT? PUZZLE 1

Which three Allied leaders met in Tehran in November 1943, to sort out plans for the post-war world?

Churchill, Roosevelt and Stalin

The 'Big Three', as they were known, met to agree on how to smash Germany. Marshal Stalin made it known that Germany would have to be divided and that he wanted frontier adjustments favourable to Russia. The Prime Minister and the President assured him that the Anglo-US invasion of France was definitely on. The aim of the three leaders was to squeeze the German armies on all fronts.

Which Conservative politician introduced the Education Act in 1944?

Richard Austen Butler

Butler was MP for Saffron Walden and Minister of Education from 1941 to 1945. The Act raised the school leaving age to 15 and then later to 16. It ensured three types of free secondary education without a means test — grammar, secondary modern and technical. Each day would begin with non-denominational collective worship. The Act also obliged local authorities to provide school playing fields, gymnasiums and swimming baths.

Who, after ranting and raving about all the lies and deceit to which he was subjected, shot himself in April 1945?

Adolf Hitler

According to survivors, just before the Russians banged on the doors of the bunker in Berlin, the Fuehrer went to his room; a few minutes later a shot was heard. He was found on a sofa, dead from a gunshot wound. Beside him was the body of Eva Braun, who had poisoned herself. Hitler had married Braun the day before. He shot himself 10 days after his fifty-sixth birthday.

PUZZLE 1 *WHO DID WHAT?*

Who become Viceroy of India in February 1947?

Lord Louis Mountbatten

Lord Louis Mountbatten was appointed Viceroy of India to oversee the transfer of power to India and Pakistan. He then became the first Governor General of the new dominion of India (1947–8).

He entered the Royal Navy as a cadet in 1913 and went on to distinguish himself as a destroyer leader in the Second World War. He also organized a number of successful commando raids as Chief of Combined Operations (1942). He became Supreme Commander in South-East Asia (1943) and was responsible for the defence of India and the campaign which expelled the Japanese from Burma.

Who won the world light-heavyweight boxing title in July 1948?

Freddie Mills

Mills, watched by 46,000 fans at the White City stadium, beat Gus Lesnevich on points to become undisputed world champion. Two years earlier, Lesnevich had beaten Mills at London's Harringay Arena, knocking him down four times in the tenth round.

David Ben-Gurion became Prime Minister of which new state, created in 1948?

Israel

In May, Ben-Gurion, a few hours before the British mandate in Palestine was due to end, became Prime Minister of a provisional government and proclaimed a Jewish state in Palestine, to be called Israel. Israel immediately revoked the 1939 British law which limited immigration and opened its doors to all Jewish immigrants. There was a pledge of social and political equality for all, and equal rights for Arab inhabitants.

The price of a drink

Most imports of alcohol stopped after 1941. The production of beer was reduced by 5 per cent and whisky by 66 per cent. Before the war, a pint of beer cost about 6d. By 1944, the price had risen to 1s 3d a pint. Spirits had doubled, often costing as much as 25s 9d a bottle or 1s 6d a nip. This was partly due to successive budgets. Sometimes higher prices were asked for, and paid.

With a meal, in 1943, you could buy a bottle of claret for about £3 or a bottle of vodka to take away for £2 2s. However, whisky was the most sought-after.

Many pubs did not open until about 8pm, or only on alternate nights. Frequently, customers were rationed to a pint each. Glasses, too, were in short supply: customers who wanted to be served learned to bring their own.

The beer shortage was at its height in 1943. Guinness was very exclusive and bottled beer was more scarce than draught.

Fashions

Severe restraints were put on buying clothes for either sex because of rationing. Women did without stockings as much as possible. The price of the clothes was less important than the number of coupons required.

'Utility' was the trade mark on wartime clothes. There was very little variation in styles. For women, it was a period of uni-forms, overalls and sensible dress. Skirts were slightly below the knee and there was a square-shouldered, military look for coats. Slacks were practical, and some women wore mannish suits.

After the war this changed and a more feminine look was in — sloping shoulders and slim waists. Hats were small and tilted on top of hair drawn back to form a high coil.

Man-made fibres started to become popular, although many people grumbled that the early nylon garments were non-absorbent and too transparent.

PUZZLE 2 SCRAMBLE

CAN YOU LINK THE PERSON NAMED WITH THE BOOK, FILM, MUSIC, SPORT OR SUBJECT?

Fredric March	Cricket
Gussie Moran	Hamlet
Henry Moore	White Christmas
Joyce Cary	The Best Years of Our Lives
Denis Compton	Yankee Doodle Dandee
Vera Lynn	Tennis
Evelyn Waugh	The Horse's Mouth
Humphrey Bogart	'We'll Meet Again'
Norman Mailer	Casablanca
James Cagney	Brideshead Revisited
Bing Crosby	The Naked and the Dead
Laurence Olivier	Art

Fredric March

The Best Years of Our Lives (1946)

This popular film, based on a poem, depicts the return home of three American soldiers from the Second World War and how they adjust to a changed life. It won Academy awards for best picture, best director, best music score, best actor, best supporting actor, best newcomer and best editing. It also starred Myrna Loy, Dana Andrews and Virginia Mayo. The setting, Boone City, could be a town anywhere. The three heroes are a middle-aged sergeant, an airforce captain and a naval rating with articulated hooks instead of hands.

When first put on television in 1964 in the UK, the film was watched by 72 per cent of the population.

Gussie Moran

Tennis

This American tennis player, headlined as 'Gorgeous Gussie', hit the news in 1949 for appearing on the staid courts of Wimbledon wearing lace-trimmed panties, which peeped from beneath a white dress. Press photographers nearly rioted trying to get photographs of her. There was also a row between the disapproving members of the All-England Club and the designer of her outfits (Teddy Tinling).

Henry Moore

Art

In 1940 Henry Moore became an official war artist. He was one of some 30 artists employed to record the Second World War. He produced the best known results, depicting people sheltering from raids on the London Underground platforms, wrapped in blankets. The people in them looked like mummified dummies. Other artists were Paul Marsh (Battle of Britain), Graham Sunderland (romantic street scenes of the Blitz), Stanley Spencer (shipbuilding on the Clyde) and Dame Laura Knight (women at war).

Joyce Cary

The Horse's Mouth (1944)

The Horse's Mouth was one of a trilogy of novels. The other two are *Herself Surprised* (1941) and *To be a Pilgrim* (1942).

Herself Surprised is the story of Sara, a servant in a rich house, who becomes the mistress of a gifted painter, Gully Jimson. *To Be a Pilgrim* is Wilcher's story. He was going to marry Sara before she was sent to prison for stealing. *The Horse's Mouth* is Gully Jimson's story. He has just come out of prison and has no scruples about anything except the pursuit of his art.

Denis Compton

Cricket

In 1947, Compton made the record aggregate of 3,816 runs and 18 hundreds in a season. He was distinguished by his cavalier style, which attracted the crowds. He also played football, playing left-wing for Arsenal. He represented England in 10 wartime internationals and in the Victory International versus Scotland in 1946.

Vera Lynn

'We'll Meet Again' (1941)

Vera Lynn was known as 'the Forces' Sweetheart'. The song 'We'll Meet Again' was the signature tune for her radio programme, 'Sincerely Yours'. Initially, the BBC and the War Office objected to her sentimental lyrics, stating that her 'crooning, drivelling and slush' would sap the fighting spirit of the forces. They thought that military marches should be played instead. How wrong can you be!

Evelyn Waugh

Brideshead Revisited (1945)

The author said, in a 1960 preface, that the novel was 'an attempt to trace the awakenings of the divine purpose in a pagan world'. Some critics saw it as an account of emotional surrender by a man, Charles Ryder, who finds reality too harsh to deal with.

Waugh said that he had wasted his time at Oxford. He taught in private schools and was dismissed from one of them for drunkenness. His other novels include *Black Mischief* (1932), *Scoop* (1938) and *Put Out More Flags* (1942).

Humphrey Bogart

Casablanca (1942)

Humphrey Bogart, or 'Bogey', has cult status. He was the tough guy with integrity, the sort of guy you would want to have around when the going gets tough. His role as Rick in the film *Casablanca* reflected his own image of being worldly wise with a heart of gold under the veneer of cynicism. His speech in the last scene of the film has been a favourite with impersonators ever since: "It doesn't take a genius to figure that the problems of three little people don't amount to a hill of beans in this crazy world." Bogart married four times. His last wife was Lauren Bacall.

Norman Mailer

The Naked and the Dead (1948)

Mailer served in the US army and afterwards wrote his best-selling novel, *The Naked and the Dead*, which was based on his war experience. It is also an abrasive comment on American society. This theme appears again in his other books, *Barbary Shore* (1951) and *The Deer Park* (1955).

James Cagney

Yankee Doodle Dandee (1942)

This film was based on the life of the playwright, actor and producer, George M. Cohan. James Cagney, playing Cohan, won an Oscar for best actor. The dance numbers in the film went into the Hollywood Hall of Fame and, of their kind, have not been excelled since. The film was also known for the large number of American patriotic songs which were worked into the production, including Cohan's:

> Over there, over there!
> Send the word, send the word, over there!
> For the Yanks are coming, the Yanks are coming,
> The drums rum-tumming everywhere ...

At this time the real war was raging in Europe and America was volunteering to help.

Bing Crosby

White Christmas (1942)

Written by Irving Berlin, 'White Christmas' was one of the most popular songs ever written, and Crosby was one of the most popular entertainers of all time. His pre-eminence as a star on radio, records and film was not seriously challenged until Frank Sinatra arrived on the scene. Crosby won an Oscar for his portrayal of a Catholic priest in *Going My Way* (1944). He cultivated an 'ordinary fella' approach, which made it all look easy. He died in 1977 while playing golf — one of his favourite relaxations.

Laurence Olivier

Hamlet (1948)

This black-and-white film won Academy Awards for best film, best actor, best art director and best costume design. Olivier starred in and directed it, winning both Oscars. The cast also included Jean Simmons, Peter Cushing and Anthony Quayle. Olivier saw the film as an attempt to bring Shakespeare to the people by bringing it down to bare melodramatic essentials.

What was on the radio

In 1940, regional broadcasts were severely reduced. The 'Forces' programmes that year provided light entertainment for both troops and workers. At the end of the war, in 1945, the Home Service and the Light Programme began. In 1946, the more intellectual Third Programme was established. One use of music broadcasts, introduced during the Second World War, was to play 'music while you work' to lighten the mechanical, repetitive work in munition factories.

'The Brains Trust', at first known as 'Any Questions', began in January 1941 as a programme for serious-minded members of the forces, but was quickly repeated on the Home Service. The programme was listened to by one in three of the adult population. There was a panel of three resident members and one visitor, who were asked questions on a wide variety of subjects. Professor Joad, who was the anchor man in the show, was so popular he had to be escorted to public meetings by the police. His reputation, however, was ruined in1948, when he was convicted for travelling without a railway ticket.

In December 1941, Dorothy L. Sayers provoked a controversy with her religious series, 'The Man Born To Be King'. The Lord's Day Observance Society denounced Broadcasting House as 'a temple of blasphemy'.

'Saturday Night Theatre' began in 1943. Another series was the American-style thriller, 'Appointment With Fear'. This starred Valentine Dyall as the sinister Man in Black.

'Workers' Playtime' was broadcast three times a week in the dinner-hour. 'Sandy's Half-Hour' linked servicemen and their families by playing requests. Most wartime children must remember Children's Hour and 'Uncle Mac', who compered the show, and his last words every evening: "Good night children, everywhere."

'Hi-Gang' starred Bebe Daniels and Ben Lyon. Also, Richard Murdoch and Kenneth Horne started making their reputations in 1944, with 'Much-Binding-in-the-Marsh'.

PUZZLE 3 *WHAT HAPPENED?*

What dramatic event of The Second World War took place between 27 May and 4 June 1940?

The evacuation of Dunkirk

The British and the French were driven back to the coast by a German force of 750,000. The surrender of Belgium had allowed the Germans to advance through a gap between the French and British lines. The British government did not think they could get more than 45,000 troops away from Dunkirk but in the event over 300,000 were rescued in 'Operation Dynamo'. All sorts of craft took part: destroyers, ferries, fishing boats and river cruisers. The German advance was also slowed down by flooding the surrounding low-lying fields and blowing bridges over the many canals in the area.

What happened to the 'unsinkable' German ship, Bismarck, *in the Atlantic in May 1941?*

She was sunk

The *Bismarck*, a 45,000-ton battleship, was pursued by around 100 British vessels determined to avenge the sinking of the British ship, HMS *Hood*. The *Bismarck* was chased for 1,750 miles, from Greenland to 550 miles west of Land's End, as she tried to reach safety in the port of Brest. She was bombed by aircraft from the *Ark Royal* and finished off by the battleships *Rodney*, *King George V* and a torpedo strike from HMS *Victorious*.

What happened to the US Pacific Fleet in Pearl Harbor on 7 December 1941?

It was attacked by the Japanese

A few hours later, Japan announced it was at war with the United States and Britain. The US Navy was caught completely unawares, and within two hours five battleships, 14 smaller ships and 1200 aircraft had been sunk or seriously damaged. Fortunately, two aircraft carriers were out of the harbour at the time.

WHAT HAPPENED? PUZZLE 3

What happened in Cologne on 30 May 1942?

It was bombed by around 1,000 Allied bombers

Royal Air Force chiefs claimed to have destroyed more than 200 factories in the raid. Over 2,000 tons of bombs were said to have been dropped. The scale of the attack was reported to have been more than four times greater than the worst raid on London, on 16 April 1941. The idea was to disrupt the German economy and destroy morale.

What happened to the Möhne and the Eder Dams in May 1943?

Both dams were bombed by the Dam Busters

The raids were carried out by specially fitted Lancaster bombers of 617 Squadron, led by Wing Commander Guy Gibson. The pilots flew in low and dropped specially designed 'bouncing bombs', which skimmed over the surface of the water and then sank before exploding at the front of the dams. The Eder Dam, the largest in Europe, holding back a 17-mile reservoir, was destroyed and a 100-yard breach was opened up in the Möhne Dam. The raids caused massive damage to industry.

What happened to the south of Moscow in July 1943, involving tanks?

The greatest tank battle in history

The battle was fought on the flat cornlands around Kursk. Hitler, after disaster at Stalingrad, launched an offensive which he said 'would shine like a beacon around the world'. He hoped that it would show the whole world that resistance to the German army was useless. However, the Russians were fully prepared for the attack and Hitler suffered a massive defeat.

PUZZLE 3 *WHAT HAPPENED?*

Which historic event took place on 6 June 1944?

The D-day landings at Normandy in France
This was the biggest combined land, sea and air operation of all time. Throughout the night RAF bombers pounded German batteries; then, at daybreak, more than 1,300 heavy bombers from the US airforce took over the attack. The seaborne force comprised several thousand ships, converging on the invasion coast just after 5am. Battleships out at sea and destroyers closer in to land pounded the German defences. By nightfall the Prime Minister was able to make a statement that the Allied forces had penetrated several miles inland on a broad front.

What event was celebrated on 16 August 1945?

The Japanese surrender
Britain's part in the war had been only a few days short of six years. Peace was celebrated by two days' public holiday and a broadcast by the King. Mr Attlee announced on the radio: "Japan has today surrendered. The last of our enemies is laid low." In America, President Truman said: "This is the day we have been waiting for since Pearl Harbor."

What happened to Hermann Goering in October 1946?

He committed suicide
Goering organized the Gestapo and set up the first concentration camps. Documents in the Nuremberg trial revealed the large part he played in preparing the war and proved his knowledge of and complicity in the atrocities committed by the Nazi regime. He and 10 other war criminals were sentenced to death, but he managed to commit suicide with a cyanide pill a few hours before he was due to be hanged.

WHAT HAPPENED? PUZZLE 3

What happened to the coal industry in January 1947?

It was nationalized

The pits came under the ownership of the National Coal Board from 1 January 1947. However, miners' leaders, after struggling for years for improved conditions, were unconvinced about the new deal. Many remained suspicious of their new employers. Emmanuel Shinwell, the Minister for Fuel, warned: "The promised five-day week for miners is difficult. Coal exports are down to vanishing point."

What happened at the Oval on 14 August 1948 to the great Australian cricketer, Donald Bradman?

He was bowled out for a duck

Australia had been dominating the final test when Bradman went in to bat in his last test match, to a standing ovation. He was bowled out by the second ball — a googly — from Eric Hollies.

If Bradman had managed to score a mere four runs it would have given him a test average of over 100 per innings.

What world sporting event took place in London in August 1948?

The Olympic Games

This was the first Olympics since the Berlin games 12 years earlier. Despite post-war austerity and the absence of Germany, the Soviet Union and Japan, the games were very successful. The organizers utilized old venues as there was no money available to build new arenas. The Americans dominated the events, winning 38 gold medals. Britain's three golds were in rowing (2) and yachting (1). A notable performance came from a 17-year-old American, Bob Mathias, who won the decathlon.

Red petrol

There was a drastic cut in the use of petrol for private cars. Petrol intended for commercial use was dyed red so that the system could not be abused. Any private motorist found with red petrol in his tank was summoned. An undercover service sprang up in which law-breakers bleached red petrol and sold it for around £1 a gallon.

Prefabricated houses

In April 1944, the first of 500,000 prefabricated houses went on show in London. They were designed for demobilized servicemen and bombed-out families. The steel-built, single-storey buildings were highly praised. The 'prefabs' covered 616 square feet, had two bedrooms, a living room, bathroom, lavatory and a kitchen — a single unit comprising a washbasin, cooking stove, draining boards and refrigerator.

The world's first jet airliner

On 27 July 1949, the De Havilland Comet, the world's first jet airliner, made its maiden flight. It was flown by Group Captain John Cunningham. Later, it went into commercial service.

Mr Chad

Mr Chad was a plump-faced, long-nosed cartoon figure looking over a wall and making some remark about an item which was in short supply: "Wot no ...!" He was drawn everywhere, as most items were in short supply at one time or another.

Spoons were known to be tied to the counter in station buffets. Often the only crockery available was thick, white, crudely designed and cups were frequently without handles. Saucepans were also scarce, as were frying pans. Wallpaper disappeared — people decorated their homes with ceiling whitening or distemper.

A lack of rubber for elastic presented a serious annoyance for women. A government leaflet in 1945 advised: 'Elastic is scarce and still on war service. When your suspenders wear out cut away the worn part and replace with an inch or two of strong tape or braid. Save spare parts ... Never throw away an old corset.'

TRUE OR FALSE? PUZZLE 4

In 1940, women war workers were campaigning for the government to give them equal pay and conditions with men.

True

In January 1940, leading women's groups met in London to condemn practices which involved prejudice and unfairness. They condemned wage cuts and worsening conditions as employers tried to use the high level of female unemployment to reduce wages. They also called for women to be trained as factory supervisors in preparation for the intake of women into the war industries.

Lord Tweedsmuir, the Governor-General of Canada, was also known as John Buchan.

True

John Buchan died on 11 February 1940, aged 64. Most people remember him as a writer and the creator of Richard Hannay, the hero of *The Thirty-Nine Steps*, *Greenmantle* and *The Three Hostages*. He was, in his lifetime, also a Scottish MP, head of Reuters and a Lord High Commissioner of the Church of Scotland. His autobiography, *Memory Hold the Door*, was published in 1940.

He was made a peer in 1935 and succeeded Lord Bessborough as Governor-General of Canada.

The Daily Worker *newspaper was encouraged by the Home Secretary, in January 1941, to keep going during the war.*

False

The government actually decided to suppress the *Daily Worker* and banned publication of the newspaper. Herbert Morrison, the Minister for Home Security, said it was constantly agitating against the war. He feared that it might begin to undermine public morale. This came about because, after air-raids, representatives of the newspaper gave out leaflets telling people whose homes had been damaged that the war was a plot to make profit for the capitalists.

Some public baths and baths in hotels had 'plimsoll lines' drawn on them to discourage people from using too much hot water.

True

The population was urged to take fewer baths in 1942 and to use no more than 5 inches of hot water when they did. This was to save fuel, which was in short supply. Shared baths were also encouraged.

The 'Bevin Boys' were men taken from the coal mines to go to war.

False

The Minister of Labour, Ernest Bevin, in 1943 introduced a scheme under which one out of every 10 men between the ages of 18 and 25 called up to go into the forces was ordered instead to work in the coal mines. This was because of manpower shortages. The conscripted miners were called the 'Bevin Boys'. The government said at the time that the mixing of the classes in the coalfields would be good for democracy.

Field Marshal Erwin Rommel shot himself in October 1944, after taking part in the July plot to get rid of Adolf Hitler.

False

Rommel committed suicide by taking poison. The Nazis issued a statement saying that he died from injuries after his car was attacked by RAF planes. The truth, however, was that Rommel knew about the plot to kill Hitler. When Hitler found out he said that, if Rommel committed suicide, he would have a hero's funeral; if he did not, he would face the 'People's Court'. Rommel chose suicide.

William Joyce was also known as Lord Haw Haw.

True

Joyce was employed by the Germans to broadcast anti-British propaganda. People were amused rather than alarmed and there was a lot of speculation about the identity of Lord Haw Haw — a nickname given to him because of the way he spoke. Joyce was arrested after the war, tried for treason at the Old Bailey in 1946 and later executed.

The American General, George S. Patton, died in action a few days before the war ended.

False

'Old Blood and Guts' Patton, as he was known, died on 21 December 1945 in a hospital in Heidelberg, Germany, after the war had ended. He had been in a car accident and had suffered chest injuries. He was one of the most successful and colourful generals of the war and was once temporarily relieved of his command for hitting a soldier whom he suspected of malingering. He was responsible for victories in North Africa and on the Western Front. He was known as a self-righteous man and was not liked by his arch-rival, the British General Montgomery.

Biro pens first went on sale in Britain in 1946.

True

The pen was invented by a Hungarian journalist, Ladislao Biro. He had been fascinated by printers' quick-drying ink when he was in Budapest. He fled to Argentina to escape the Nazis and sold out in 1944 to his English backer, H G Martin, who began marketing the pens. The revolutionary new pen was said to write 200,000 words without having to be refilled and without blotting or smudging and cost 55 shillings.

PUZZLE 4 *TRUE OR FALSE?*

In November 1947, Chuck Yeager, an American test pilot, was the first man to travel faster than sound.

True

He flew from a base in California in a Bell X-1 rocket plane. Travelling at over 600mph he broke through the sound barrier with a loud noise like a clap of thunder.

The National Health Service came into being on 5 July 1949.

False

It came into being on 5 July 1948 and was regarded as the most sweeping reform ever. It included a national insurance scheme and welfare systems dealing with unemployment and old people. The Health Service offered free medical treatment for the entire population, free prescriptions, free dental care, free glasses and wigs under prescription.

At that time, the Health Minister, Aneurin Bevan, faced powerful opposition from the British Medical Association and doctors when he began negotiations. However, he estimated that some 19,000 doctors would have accepted the service by the end of the first week.

Clothes rationing ended on 15 March 1949.

True

Clothes rationing had been imposed in 1941. However, after 15 March 1949, the utility scheme continued — ready-to-wear clothes were made under a clothes quota system. Also, price controls remained as the government wanted to be able to freeze prices if traders started to increase them too much.

Going to the cinema

At the beginning of the war all cinemas closed by government order. This was changed, but performances finished by 11pm. It was not until 1942 that the pre-war habit of weekly cinema-going was restored. Cinemas also opened on Sundays to cater for soldiers and war workers away from home. More people than ever packed in to see films.

Flashes would appear on the screen, or the manager would come on stage, to say that the sirens were going and offer refunds to people who wanted to leave. Later, most cinemas had red, lighted signs fitted beside the screen which gave a warning when air-raids were beginning. At first, most people left, but later most stopped to see the rest of the film and took the risk. If bombs were still falling at the end of a performance some managers allowed audiences to stay, frequently showing the whole programme again.

Cinema programmes were longer than ever. There was a supporting 'B' film, a newsreel and at least one official film on subjects like salvage or careless talk. There were many films being shown. *The Way Ahead* (1944) starred David Niven and described how a group of men from many different walks of life were moulded together into a fighting unit. *This Happy Breed* (1944) was about a typical working-class family's reaction to war.

A number of the films being shown were based on British history; they included *The Young Mr Pitt*, with Robert Donat in the title role, *The Prime Minister*, starring John Gielgud and *Lady Hamilton*, starring Vivien Leigh.

Other films shown during the forties included *Jamaica Inn*, *Goodbye Mr Chips*, *The Stars Look Down*, *Kipps*, *The Man in Grey*, *The Next of Kin*, *We Dive at Dawn*, *49th Parallel*, *The Way to the Stars*, *Thunder Rock*, *Mrs Miniver*, *Blithe Spirit*, *The Third Man*, *Brief Encounter*, *Notorious* and *Passport to Pimlico*.

CAN YOU PUZZLE OUT THE CONNECTION BETWEEN THE FOLLOWING?

A fan of Hitler
Lord Redesdale
Storm Troop Maiden
A bullet in the head

Unity Mitford

Unity Mitford was one of Lord Redesdale's daughters. She was a devoted admirer of Hitler and was in the habit of sitting in a restaurant in Osteria, Bavaria, waiting to see Hitler when he came in. He did, in fact, notice her and invited her to join his table. She became known as the 'Storm Troop Maiden'. When war was declared she shot herself in the head, but not fatally. Afterwards, Hitler gave special permission for her to return home. She arrived on the ferry at Folkestone on a stretcher on 3 January 1940.

2 June 1941
Margarine coupons
Clothing

Margarine coupons were required to buy clothing

From 2 June 1941, margarine coupons could be used to buy clothes, in addition to the actual cost. This was an interim measure until clothing coupons could be printed.

A special scale was introduced to allow for growing children and people losing clothing through enemy action. Families on £4 to £5 a week were required to reduce their purchases by about a quarter, and above that wage by more.

The Board Of Trade took the advice of three women on the amount of clothing required by a woman during a year — one was a business woman, another a housewife and the third a buyer for a company.

Unmarried women between 20 and 30
Anti-aircraft crews/desk jobs

Conscription for women

Owing to manpower shortages in the Forces and in factories it was decided in 1941 that all single women between 20 and 30 years old should be called up. Some served in anti-aircraft crews with men; others were designated desk jobs previously filled by medically fit men.

WHAT'S THE CONNECTION? PUZZLE 5

Hong Kong
Christmas Day 1941
Britain

Britain surrendered Hong Kong to the Japanese

The British force surrendered unconditionally after a seven-day battle. They were hopelessly outnumbered, about 6,000 defenders against two entire Japanese divisions estimated at 40,000 men, and were down to a 24-hour supply of water. This was part of a massive Japanese offensive in the Pacific and South-East Asia which started with the attack on Pearl Harbor on 7 December 1941.

George Cross
An island fortress in the Mediterranean
April 1942

The George Cross was awarded to the people of Malta

Malta presented a threat to the German lines of communication with Rommel in North Africa. The Germans tried to bomb the island into submission. In a period of four months, Malta had over 1,000 day and night raids and alerts. There were almost daily air battles. The Royal Navy tried hard to get supplies through to the island but most attempts failed. King George said, in a message to the Governor-General, Sir William Dobie, that the 'heroism and devotion' of a brave people 'will long be famous in history'.

Nazis
A mine on the Laser Plateau in Austria
15 April 1945

Priceless art treasures were found

The Nazis had looted art treasures and deposited them in the mine. The loot included pictures by Rembrandt, Rubens, Leonardo da Vinci, Raphael, Goya and Michelangelo. The Nazis had ordered a Dr Wilhelm, a director of the Vienna Museum, to live in the mine and look after the paintings. The mine was wired up with bombs so that everything could be destroyed. Orders were given to SS troops to detonate them, but Dr Wilhelm, with the aid of Free Austria workers, cut the fuse wires and blew up the entrance to the shaft, thus saving the paintings.

PUZZLE 5 *WHAT'S THE CONNECTION?*

An American plane named 'Enola Gay'
Japan
6 August 1945

The atomic bomb dropped on Hiroshima

The 'Enola Gay' was a Superfortress aircraft named after the mother of the pilot. Concussion from the blast of the bomb struck the plane 10 miles away. It was reported that four hours after the explosion nothing could be seen but the pall of smoke and fire. A few days later another bomb was dropped on Nagasaki.

India and Pakistan
Britain
15 August 1947

India and Pakistan gained independence

Britain's Indian Empire came to an end and the new dominion of Pakistan and India emerged. It was the end of 163 years of British rule. Lord Louis Mountbatten, as last Imperial Viceroy, administered the handing over of power and became India's first Governor-General.

President of the Board of Trade
Labour MP for Ormskirk
September 1947

Harold Wilson

In a ministerial reshuffle, Harold Wilson was made President of the Board of Trade. At 31, this made him the youngest member of the cabinet. After a brilliant academic career he had previously been seconded to the Ministry of Fuel and Power during the war and became Labour MP for Ormskirk in 1945.

Winter of 1947
Power cuts
RAF food drops

Snowstorms

Heavy snowstorms combined with fuel shortages to produce one of the worst winters on record. There were power cuts resulting in millions being laid off work and thousands of homes were without heat or light. Hundreds of rail and coach passengers were stranded, owing to snowdrifts. Non-stop blizzards stopped all shipping in the Channel, creating a threat to food supplies. Troops were called in to help throughout the country and the RAF dropped food to stranded villages.

Berlin
A Russian blockade
June 1948

The Berlin airlift

A round-the-clock airlift was carried out by the Western Allies in order to beat the Russian blockade of Berlin. All surface transport had been blocked. Some 200 Dakota aircraft flew from an airbase near Hanover to Berlin, taking in food and essential supplies for the Western Zones of the city. An aircraft landed every four minutes.

The Yangtse River
The frigate HMS Amethyst
July 1949

HMS *Amethyst* made a dash for freedom

After being shelled by the Chinese Communist armies, the *Amethyst* had been trapped for four months. The frigate then made a 140-mile dash, under the cover of darkness, down the Yangtse river. She was shelled by Chinese batteries and broke through a river boom to reach safety. The Commander, Lieutenant-Commander J.S. Kerans, was awarded the DSO.

DO YOU REMEMBER?

Paper shortages

Paper shortages affected the production of books and newspapers. Books became thinner and had narrower margins, smaller type and a note on the front: 'This book is produced in complete conformity with the authorised economic standards.' Forewords, introductions and chapters ran on, so that it was difficult to know where one ended and the other began. The number of new books published went down from 15,000 in 1939 to 6,700 in 1943, where it remained until after the war.

The shortage was hard on newspapers: they, too, became thinner. Trade was bad and advertising hard to encourage. Before the war the *Daily Express* had 16, 20 or 24 pages, but by 1941 it was producing four pages — one double sheet. Smaller-sized newspapers like the *Daily Mirror* and the *Evening Standard* had eight pages, as did *The Times* which also occasionally managed to run to 10 or 12 pages.

Heating, kitchens and bathrooms

After 1945, there was a wider choice of domestic water heaters. Most old-style kitchen ranges connected with the boiler were replaced by up-to-date cooker heaters such as Agas or Rayburns before 1950. These could be kept going night and day and had low fuel consumption. Their vitreous enamel, wipe-clean surfaces were very popular with housewives after the old, blackened ranges.

Some very efficient gas and electric heaters were available. These were fitted as water heaters over kitchen sinks or the bath in houses with no circulating hot-water systems. Also common in 1948 was a back-boiler behind the lounge fireplace, for use in winter. An electric immersion heater in the hot-water tank was used in the summer when there was no fire.

The baby boom

In 1947, the birth-rate soared — the highest for 26 years! The abnormally high number of births was thought to be caused by many couples catching up on the lost war years.

FAMOUS PEOPLE CROSSWORD

DRAW THIS CROSSWORD ON A BLACKBOARD, PHOTOCOPY THIS PAGE AND GIVE IT TO EACH PERSON, OR USE THE CLUES AS A STRAIGHT QUIZ

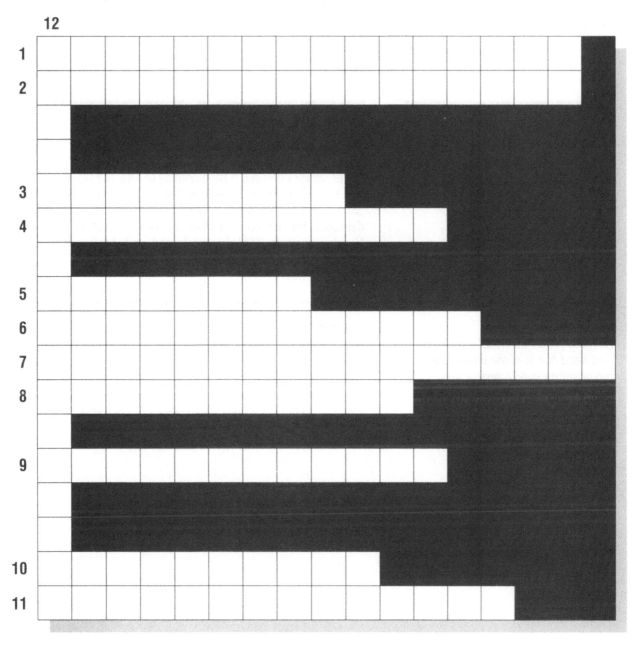

1 ACROSS

*He laid the foundation for the
Welfare State and was known as
the 'Welsh Wizard'.*

2 ACROSS

*He became Prime Minister in
May 1940.*

3 ACROSS

*He mass-produced Model-T cars and
was head of one of the world's largest
motor-car manufacturers.*

David Lloyd-George

David Lloyd-George died on 26 March 1945 at the age of 82. He was a social reformer and a great orator. During the First World War he was an inspiring war leader. However, he was undoubtedly responsible for much bitterness and a rift in the Liberal Party from which it never recovered. He was Prime Minister from 1916 to 1922.

Winston Churchill

Winston Churchill was a politician, author and painter. Before the war he bitterly opposed the policy of appeasement. When made Prime Minister he said, "I have nothing to offer but blood, toil, tears and sweat." As Prime Minister he led a coalition government with Labour and Liberal support. After the war, in 1945, his party was defeated, but he continued as leader and resumed as Prime Minister again in 1951–5. A colourful and controversial figure, Churchill inspired the confidence of the nation with his leadership during the war.

Henry Ford

Henry Ford died on 7 April 1947 during a power cut caused by floods in Detroit. He was 83. He built his first two-cylinder bicycle-wheel car in 1896 while working for Edison in Detroit and set up the Ford Motor Company in 1904. He was a tough but peculiar man, who paid his workers high wages but resisted trade unions. He said: "History is bunk", but built a vast historical collection.

FAMOUS PEOPLE CROSSWORD PUZZLE 6

4 ACROSS

He starred in the film Brief Encounter *(1945).*

Trevor Howard

This famous film, also starring Celia Johnson and Stanley Holloway, was directed by David Lean. Post-war austerity was the keynote in this love story: Celia Johnson is apprehensive when Trevor Howard borrows a friend's flat for some adulterous love-making. Lovers, in the movies, were still discreet in 1945.

5 ACROSS

She married Juan Peron who, in 1946, was made President of Argentina, and she became known as 'Evita'.

Eva Peron

Eva Peron was a small-part actress on radio and in films. She met Juan Peron in 1943 and married him in 1945. Army leaders feared her and tried to force her out of public life. There was good reason, as she wielded enormous power, effectively running both the Health and Labour Ministries as well as controlling the leading newspaper, *La Razon*. She also ran the Eva Peron Social Aid Foundation, which channelled state funds to the poor. Her popularity with labourers helped Juan Person make his successful bid for the Presidency. He relied on her to organize popular demonstrations to support him when he needed to counter army power.

6 ACROSS

A Swedish actress who won an Oscar for her role in Gaslight *in 1944.*

Ingrid Bergman

Ingrid Bergman became Hollywood's top female star in the forties and was usually cast as a woman suffering for love. Other films included *Casablanca* (1942), *For Whom the Bell Tolls* (1943), *Spellbound* (1945) and *Joan of Arc* (1948)

PUZZLE 6 *FAMOUS PEOPLE CROSSWORD*

7 ACROSS
A world-famous composer who wrote 'Rhapsody on a Theme of Paganini' and was equally famous as a pianist.

8 ACROSS
In 1940, he was made Minister for Labour; in 1945, he became Foreign Secretary and was MP for Central Wandsworth.

9 ACROSS
He became President of the USA in April 1945, after the sudden death of President Roosevelt.

Sergei Rachmaninov

As a pianist he was in the first rank. He studied at St Petersburg and the Moscow Conservatoire where he formed a friendship with Tchaikovsky. After the Russian revolution he lived in the USA, but travelled widely in Europe. He died at his home in Beverly Hills on 28 March 1943, aged 69. His last work was his Symphonic Dances (1940).

Ernest Bevin

Bevin's achievements included uniting 32 separate unions into the huge Transport and General Workers' Union. He was the son of an agricultural labourer and worked as a van boy and driver. He became MP for Central Wandsworth in 1940 and remained until 1950. He was one of the architects of the Brussels Treaty (1948) and NATO (1949).

Harry S Truman

Harry Truman authorized the use of the atomic bomb against Japan in August 1945. In 1948, he was elected President, which he considered a personal triumph. Despite the fact that all the pollsters had forecast a massive win for his opponent, Thomas E. Dewey, Truman won by two million votes.

Truman was a man of honour. After the First World War, a business venture he was involved in failed but he insisted on paying the creditors in full, an effort which took him 15 years. When he assumed office, not much was expected of him, but he became one of America's great Presidents.

FAMOUS PEOPLE CROSSWORD **PUZZLE 6**

10 ACROSS

A great swashbuckling American film star who was charged and acquitted of statutory rape in 1943.

Errol Flynn

Flynn was a renowned womanizer on and off the screen. He was accused of interfering with 17-year-old Betty Hansen at a dinner party on October 1942, and Peggy La Rue Satterlee accused him of attacking her on board his yacht. Flynn's reputation as a lover and star was only enhanced by the trial. He was also accused of being a Nazi spy, an IRA supporter and a freedom fighter for Castro. Perhaps Flynn was not the only one having difficulty telling the difference between reality and the movies!

11 ACROSS

He composed the music for Oklahoma (1943) with lyricist Oscar Hammerstein II.

Richard Rodgers

Richard Rodgers composed musical comedies for film and stage. In the 1920s he began his career with lyricist Lorenz Hart. One of their productions was the very popular *Pal Joey* (1940). Hart died in 1943 and Rodgers started collaborating with Oscar Hammerstein. *Oklahoma* was one of their greatest successes. It ran for five years on Broadway and made a profit of seven million dollars.

12 DOWN

In 1943, he was appointed Supreme Commander of Allied Forces engaged in the liberation of Western Europe.

Dwight D. Eisenhower

"Everyone likes Ike", it was said about this man. He could, in fact, be warm and outgoing but also cold and ungenerous. His organizing ability contributed to the success of the landings and the ensuing battle of Normandy. He became President of the USA in 1953.

the 1950s

ALTHOUGH THE Second World War was over, peace still eluded the world. This was the decade of Korea, the French war in Vietnam and Suez; and the cold war between East and West continued.

In America the fifties saw extraordinary witch-hunts against Communists and Communist sympathizers. No walk of life escaped: movie actors, writers, scientists and members of the armed forces all appeared before the Permanent Subcommittee on Investigations. These witch-hunts were led by Senator Joseph McCarthy of Wisconsin.

Kenya saw violence as the Mau Mau acted to drive the white man out of the country. In Cyprus, EOKA terrorists killed many people in the cause of obtaining freedom from British rule.

At home the hovercraft, invented by Christopher Cockerell, came into being. On 28 June 1950, in the first round of the World Cup, England lost 1–0 to the USA. The BBC announced in January 1951: "People do not like momentous events such as war and disaster to be read by the female voice." In January 1951, rump steak was on sale at 2s 8d a pound.

The fifties saw a revolution in fashion. Clothes became much more varied. A new type of adolescent began to emerge. The expression 'teenager' was introduced from America. Rock 'n roll had an enormous impact. In some cinemas where the film *Rock Around the Clock* was showing, audiences 'rocked' in the aisles.

Towards the end of the decade, the 'Edwardian' craze set in. 'Teddyboys' and 'Teddygirls' were frequently in the news. Unfortunately, their behaviour often annoyed and soured public opinion.

The car industry revived and sales of private cars began to soar. Power supplies reached remote areas and increasing prosperity was shown by the large number of people who now had washing machines, refrigerators and television sets.

In 1957, the Prime Minister, Harold Macmillan, said: "Let us be frank about it. Most of our people have never had it so good." He asked his party to rejoice over the improvement in standards of living. Instead of austerity, he said, there was an abundance of goods and freedom of choice.

WHO DID WHAT? PUZZLE 1

NAME THE PERSON OR PERSONS INVOLVED IN THE FOLLOWING EVENTS

Who was the Norwegian anthropologist whose book The Kon-Tiki Expedition *was published in March 1950?*

Thor Heyerdahl

Thor Heyerdahl made a 5,000-mile journey across the Pacific on a raft to settle an argument. He believed that Polynesian islanders originally sailed from Peru in South America to Polynesia, suggesting that Peruvian indians could have settled in Polynesia. Experts said that such a journey was impossible. Heyerdahl set out to prove them wrong. He set off, in 1948, with five crewmen, on a raft made of balsa logs roped together, on a journey that lasted 101 days. The book tells the story of how he proved his point.

Which screen star, on the occasion of her marriage to Nicky Hilton on 6 May 1950, said: "I just love everything about getting married" and has since proved her point by getting married nine times?

Elizabeth Taylor

At the height of her career, Taylor was the highest paid star of them all. She was born in England of American parents and became famous as a child star during the Second World War, appearing in *Lassie Come Home* and *National Velvet*. In the fifties her films included *A Place in the Sun* (1951), *Giant* (1956) and *Cat on a Hot Tin Roof* (1958). She was dubbed the world's most beautiful woman. In later years she has become known for her battle with health problems, involvement in political issues and charitable causes, rather than acting.

Which American singer began his career with the Tommy Dorsey band and made his first appearance at the London Palladium in July 1950?

Frank Sinatra

When he appeared at the London Palladium, Sinatra had just out-done Bing Crosby as the highest paid singer in the USA by signing a radio contract worth one million pounds. Not all the critics were kind to his London show. One reported: "You can hear every word he sings which is sometimes a pity, considering his material." In 1953, he won an Oscar for his role in the film *From Here to Eternity*. The film *Pal Joey* (1957) was another big success for him in the fifties.

PUZZLE 1 *WHO DID WHAT?*

Which two British diplomats went missing in May 1951 in circumstances which led to their being suspected of spying?

Donald Maclean and Guy Burgess

Both men, diplomats serving in sensitive posts in the Washington embassy, were suspected of being undercover Soviet spies. On 8 June, a telegram from them said that they were taking a long Mediterranean holiday. London played the issue down, but American newspapers highlighted the event. Of course, we now know that they had been passing on information.

Which British boxer beat Sugar Ray Robinson to win the world middleweight title in July 1951?

Randolph Turpin

Turpin became the first British fighter to hold the title since Bob Fitzsimmons the previous century. Against all prediction, he won the fight on points at Earls Court. Before the fight, bookmakers were offering 3–1 against Turpin and as much as 20–1 against his winning on points.

Who was 'Singin' in the Rain' in the film of the same name in 1952?

Gene Kelly

This film is said by some to be the best musical ever made. It also starred Donald O'Connor and Debbie Reynolds. The dance sequence, in which Kelly tap-dances and sings the title number through a downpour of rain has become one of the most famous movie sequences of all time.

Kelly, as star, choreographer and director, was the most important influence on movie musicals of his time. In 1951, he was presented with a special Oscar for his screen contribution.

Was *Singin' in the Rain* the best musical ever made? Can you think of a better one?

Which Senator, who later became President of the USA, did Jacqueline Lee Bouvier marry on 12 September 1953?

John Fitzgerald Kennedy

Previously, Jacqueline Lee Bouvier had worked as a photographer for the *Washington Times–Herald*. John Kennedy continued to make rapid political progress. He nearly won the vice-presidential nomination in 1956. In 1960, he became the Democratic candidate for the Presidency and won, becoming the youngest US president to be elected.

Which British athlete broke the four-minute mile barrier on 6 May 1954?

Roger Bannister

Bannister was a 25-year-old medical student when he became the first man to run a mile in under four minutes. It happened on the university track at Iffley Road, Oxford, in an event between the university and the Amateur Athletic Association. Bannister's time was 3 minutes 59.4 seconds. In 1954, Bannister also won the Commonwealth mile, in 3 minutes 58.8 seconds, and the European 1500m, in 3 minutes 43.8 seconds.

Which member of the royal family decided against marrying Group Captain Peter Townsend in 1955?

Princess Margaret

In October, Princess Margaret made a statement: "I would like it to be known that I have decided not to marry Group Captain Peter Townsend. I have been aware that, subject to renouncing my rights of succession, it might have been possible for me to contract a civil marriage, but mindful of the Church's teaching that Christian marriage is indissoluble and conscious of my duty to the Commonwealth, I have resolved to put these considerations above all others."

The statement ended two weeks of intense speculation. The princess could have married without the Queen's consent under the Royal Marriage Act of 1772, but would have had to wait a year. She would also have lost her payments from the Civil List and her place as third in line to the throne.

PUZZLE 1 *WHO DID WHAT?*

Who did Grace Kelly marry on 19 April 1956?

Prince Rainier III of Monaco

The ceremony took place in the clifftop cathedral of St Nicholas, Monaco. In the congregation were the Aga Khan, Ava Gardner and Aristotle Onassis. Grace Kelly gave up her career as an actress to marry the prince. Her films included *High Noon* (1952), *Dial M for Murder* (1954), *Rear Window* (1954) and *High Society* (1956).

After the ceremony the couple drove to the royal palace in a cream and black open-topped Rolls-Royce. There were an estimated 1,800 journalists staying in the principality to report the occasion, which was televised. Grace Kelly had become 'High Society' indeed.

By whom was Dr Vivian Fuchs greeted when he reached the South Pole in January 1958?

Sir Edmund Hillary

The British expedition, led by Dr Fuchs, arrived at the South Pole 17 days after their New Zealand rival, Edmund Hillary. Hillary was the first person to lead a party to the Pole overland since Captain Robert Scott, 46 years earlier.

Who became the first President of the new Republic of Cyprus in December 1959?

Archbishop Makarios

Archbishop Makarios was accused by the British in 1956 of collaborating with EOKA, the terrorist organization led by George Grivas, and was deported to the Seychelles. He was freed in 1957 and became President of the independent Republic of Cyprus in 1959. After being elected he insisted in a speech that fanaticism and antagonism must cease.

Elvis Presley

Presley fused black rhythm-and-blues with white country-and-gospel to become the greatest pop performer ever. He was born Elvis Aaron Presley in Tupelo, Mississippi, the son of a poor farm-worker and became the biggest symbol of the fifties' teenage revolt. His songs in the fifties included: 'That's All Right', 'Blue Moon of Kentucky', 'Hound Dog', 'All Shook Up' and 'Heartbreak Hotel'. He also made the films *Love Me Tender* (1956), *Loving You* (1957), *Jailhouse Rock* (1957) and *King Creole* (1958). After this, on 24 March 1958, he went into the army. Later, he made 27 more movies.

The Goon Show

'The Goon Show' started in the fifties and developed a cult follow-ing. It did not make sense, but was full of anarchic nonsense. The original Goons were Michael Bentine, Spike Milligan, Harry Secombe and Peter Sellers. They created lunatic characters like Major Bloodnok and Hercules Grytpype-Thynne, the frail and elderly lovers, Henry Crun and Minnie Bannister, and the imbeciles, Eccles and Bluebottle.

The Fishing War

In August 1958, Britain and Iceland began a fishing war over the Reykjavik government's unilateral declaration of a 12-mile fishing limit. British trawlers continued to fish off the previously accepted four-mile limit. In September 1958, two Icelandic gunboats seized a British trawler, but later had to let it go when a Royal Navy board-ing party came to the rescue. A cat-and-mouse game developed, with gunboats trying to capture any British trawlers that did not have Royal Navy protection.

Fanny Craddock

Fanny Craddock set the trend for television cooks when she began her programme, 'Kitchen Magic', on the BBC, in 1955. She appeared with her monocled husband, Johnnie, had an upper-crust accent and a hard-boiled approach. Later, she worked for both the BBC and the newly created ITV, hosting the programme, 'Fanny's Kitchen'.

PUZZLE 2 SCRAMBLE

CAN YOU LINK THE PERSON NAMED WITH THE BOOK, FILM, MUSIC, SPORT OR SUBJECT?

Charlton Heston	*Lucky Jim*
Mike Hawthorn	Tennis
Alec Guinness	Car racing
Bill Haley	*The Quiet Man*
Rodgers and Hammerstein	*Ben Hur*
Rocky Marciano	*The Bridge on the River Kwai*
Marilyn Monroe	Boxing
Kingsley Amis	*The King and I*
Len Hutton	*The Go-Between*
L.P. Hartley	*The Seven Year Itch*
Maureen Connolly (Little Mo)	'Rock Around the Clock'
John Wayne	Cricket

Charlton Heston

Ben Hur (1959)

Charlton Heston starred as Judah Ben Hur in this epic in which the ailing MGM studio invested an all-or-nothing 14.5 million dollars. Also appearing in the film were Stephen Boyd and Jack Hawkins. It is best remembered for the famous chariot race which involved weeks of arduous training for Heston and Boyd. The film won 11 Oscars in 1960, including Best Actor (Charlton Heston), Best Director and Best Picture. It also saved MGM from bankruptcy.

Mike Hawthorn

Car racing

Mike Hawthorn came to public attention in 1952 by winning two races against some of the world's leading drivers at Goodwood. Driving for Jaguar, he won at Le Mans in 1955. In October 1958, he won the World Championship by a single point from Stirling Moss. Sadly, after retiring, he was killed in January 1959 driving his own sports car on the Guildford bypass in Surrey.

Alec Guinness

The Bridge on the River Kwai (1957)

This film tells the story of the prisoners of war who built the infamous Thai–Burmese 'Death Railway' for the Japanese. It is a study of the futility of war. It also starred William Holden and Jack Hawkins. It was directed by David Lean. Alec Guinness, playing a colonel, is obsessed with building the bridge to prove the mettle of British soldiers. The film was filmed in the steamy jungles of Ceylon.

Bill Haley

'Rock Around the Clock' (1954)

Haley, a 29-year-old former country and western singer, recorded this song with the Comets in 1954. Other hits included: 'Rip it Up', 'Rockin' through the Rye' and 'Don't Knock the Rock'. Haley explained the success of rock and roll: "Its appeal is its simplicity. Everyone wants to get in on the act. With rock 'n roll, they can join in."

Rodgers and Hammerstein

The King and I (1956)

This musical film, set in the court of a despotic Oriental, starred Yul Brynner and Deborah Kerr. In the stage version, the plot was simply a battle of wills between the King and Anna, the English schoolteacher, but the film introduced a suggestion of unfulfilled love. The score included famous songs such as 'Hello, Young Lovers', 'I Whistle a Happy Tune', 'Getting to Know You', 'Shall We Dance?' and 'March of the Siamese Children'.

Rocky Marciano

Boxing

Rocky Marciano was undefeated as a professional boxer and world heavyweight champion from 1952 to 1956, when he announced his retirement. He won 49 fights, in which only five opponents managed to hear the final bell. He was the son of a New England shoemaker.

Marilyn Monroe

The Seven Year Itch (1955)

This was one of the films made by Marilyn Monroe in the fifties. Others included *The Asphalt Jungle* (1950), *Niagara* (1953), *Gentlemen Prefer Blondes* (1953) — in which she sang 'Diamonds are a Girl's Best Friend' — and *Some Like it Hot* (1959). She was born in 1926 and her real name was Norma Jean Baker. She tended to play powerless young women, which often angered feminist cinema-goers.

Kingsley Amis

Lucky Jim (1954)

This was Amis's first novel and probably the best of the 'angry young men' novels, which were popular in the late fifties. The book was a debunking of university pretentiousness. The hero, Jim Dixon, was a lecturer (like Amis) at a provincial university. The book won the Somerset Maugham Award for literature.

Len Hutton

Cricket

Len Hutton captained England 23 times between 1952 and 1954–5. He represented England in 79 out of 98 tests played between 1937 and 1954–5, scoring 6,971 runs. When playing against Australia at the Oval, in 1938, he made 364 runs — the world record Test score for the next 20 years.

PUZZLE 2 *SCRAMBLE*

L.P. Hartley

The Go-Between (1953)
This short novel, written by L.P. Hartley and set in the golden summer of 1900, tells the story of a young boy who becomes a messenger between an aristocratic young woman and her lover, a farmer. The boy's role as go-between becomes compromised because of his friendship with the woman's fiancé and the suspicions of her mother. The book was adapted and made into a film in 1971, starring Julie Christie, Alan Bates and Edward Fox.

Maureen Connolly (Little Mo)

Tennis
Maureen Connolly, known as 'Little Mo' to her fans, won the Wimbledon Singles title at her first attempt in 1952. She was 17 years old. Her opponent was the more experienced Louise Brough, who had already been champion three times since the Second World War.

John Wayne

The Quiet Man (1952)
This film saw John Wayne (the quiet man) returning home to Ireland after killing an opponent in the boxing ring in America. He falls in love with Mary Kate Danaher (Maureen O'Hara), who refuses to honour the marriage bed until her brother Will (Victor McLaglen), coughs up a dowry. The film was directed by John Ford.

Audie Murphy

Audie Murphy was America's most decorated soldier of the Second World War and a film star. It is difficult to imagine that this baby-faced man killed some 240 Germans and that he was, at the end of the war, one of only two left in his company. He called the book of his experiences *To Hell and Back* and in 1955 starred as himself in the film of the same name.

Murphy was born in 1924 and came from a poor share-cropping family in Texas. After the war, he made his name in Westerns, playing roles like Jessie James and Billy the Kid. However, his best and most successful part was that of himself in his own life story.

Debutantes

These were young women who were presented at court as a way of making their debut in society. They were the daughters of the aristocracy and others prominent in the community. Late in the fifties (1958), Buckingham Palace felt that the practice was archaic and not in touch with the times. Thus the tradition came to an end. Prince Philip was said to be influential in the decision.

To be presented at court a young woman needed a sponsor to go with her on the day. This had to be a young woman who had herself been presented. Some of these women would seek out ambitious fathers and negotiate fees to present their daughters.

Christian Dior

Christian Dior introduced his luxurious couture in Paris in 1947, and went on in the fifties to change the face of western fashion. After the mannish clothes of the war period, his 'Corrole' line (a tight bodice, shaped into a tiny waist below which a long skirt burst into fullness like a flower) was extremely feminine.

In the mid-fifties, his flat-chested 'H' line gave way to the 'A' line — still flattish, but with an easier waist, pyramid-shaped skirt and a 'wandering' belt that could be placed anywhere between mid-hip and just under the bust. Skirts were just below the knee.

Dior died on 14 October 1957, aged 52. He had first begun sketching dresses when convalescing after a serious illness. He was awarded the Legion of Honour by France for revitalizing the fashion industry: within eight years he had achieved a yearly turnover of 5 million pounds and employed 1,200 people in his subsidiaries in Paris, Britain, the USA and South America.

PUZZLE 3 *WHAT HAPPENED?*

What happened in Korea in July 1950?

North Korea invaded South Korea

Communist North Korea crossed the 38th Parallel into independent South Korea, the border agreed between the two states. The invasion came without warning. The United Nations responded by recommending that all members of the UN 'furnish such assistance to the Republic of Korea as may be necessary to meet the attack'. British troops were sent as part of this response.

What happened on the South Bank of the Thames on 3 May 1951, involving King George VI and Queen Elizabeth?

The Festival of Britain began

The Festival was opened by the King and Queen. Some 27 acres of derelict, bomb-damaged London, near Waterloo, were transformed into the exhibition site. The festival was a huge success. People went to see it from all over the country. The Festival, a government-sponsored event, was a gesture of faith in a brighter future. It was described by Herbert Morrison (Foreign Secretary) as 'the people giving themselves a pat on the back'.

What happened on 19 October 1951 in the Suez Canal Zone, involving British troops?

British troops gained control of the Canal

In 1950, King Farouk ordered the British to leave Egypt. Britain offered a Middle East pact, backed by France, Turkey and the USA, to include Egypt in a five-nation defence organization. Britain would then hand over her Egyptian base. This was rejected by Egypt. Anti-British riots broke out and led to Egypt rescinding the 1936 Anglo-Egyptian Alliance. Britain responded by occupying key points on the Suez Canal on 19 October 1951 and stopping the peace talks.

WHAT HAPPENED? PUZZLE 3

What happened in Helsinki in August 1952?

The Olympic Games

This was the Olympics in which Britain almost failed to gain any gold medals. The show-jumping team saved the day at the last minute.

The games were dominated by Emil Zatopek, a Czech, who won the 10,000 metres, 5,000 metres and the marathon, setting new Olympic records in all three events. His wife Dana also set an Olympic record for the javelin.

What happened just off Belfast Lough, on 30 January 1953?

The car ferry, *Princess Victoria*, sank

128 lives were lost as the ferry sank off Belfast Lough. At the inquest it was revealed that the ferry had left port with her cargo doors open. When a heavy wave hit the ship, water had surged in, sweeping the cargo onto the starboard side, causing the ship to list and capsize.

What happened at 10 Rillington Place, London, involving John Christie, in March 1953?

The bodies of three women were found

A new tenant found the bodies of three women hidden in the walls. A fourth body was later found under the floorboards. John Christie, the former occupier, was later charged with the murder of all four. He also confessed to three other killings, including that of Mrs Beryl Evans and her daughter. In 1950, Christie had been the Crown witness at the trial of Timothy John Evans, who was hanged for his wife's murder.

What happened in Trafalgar Square on the evening of 2 July 1954, involving rationing?

Housewives tore up their ration books

Housewives gathered in Trafalgar Square and tore up their ration books as the government announced the end of rationing, which had lasted 14 years. Ration books were also burned at a number of Conservative Association meetings.

What happened at the White City on 13 October 1954, concerning Chris Chataway?

He broke the 5,000 metres world record

The 23-year-old Oxford blue broke the record by 5 seconds, making it 13 minutes 15.6 seconds. In the process he beat the European champion Vladimir Kuts in a London versus Moscow match at White City. The race was televised.

What happened to 'Buster' Crabb in Portsmouth harbour in May 1956, involving Nikita Khrushchev?

He disappeared

Commander 'Buster' Crabb was said to be carrying out 'underwater tests' near a cruiser, on which were the visiting Soviet leaders Nikita Khrushchev and Nikolai Bulganin. The Soviets accused Britain of underwater espionage. Crabb was thought to have drowned or to be held by the Soviet navy. His headless body was found in the sea near Chichester harbour, in June 1957.

WHAT HAPPENED? PUZZLE 3

What happened in Egypt that proved humiliating for Britain in November 1956?

A military withdrawal

The US treasury had told Britain that American financial aid to prevent a total collapse of sterling depended on a British pull-out from Egypt. The British government reluctantly agreed to a military withdrawal, leaving the UN forces to go into the Suez area, maintain peace and to ensure the reopening of the Canal.

Prime Minister Sir Anthony Eden — suffering from 'severe overstrain' at the time — flew to Jamaica for a rest. Rab Butler, the Leader of the House of Commons, took temporary charge of the cabinet.

What happened on 19 July 1957, involving Derek Ibbotson from Huddersfield?

He broke the mile world record

In fact, four men broke the record, at White City, London. The other three were Ron Delany of Ireland, Stanislav Jungwirth of Czechoslovakia and Ken Wood of Sheffield. However, Ibbotson turned in the fastest time, 3 minutes 57.2 seconds. Delany was second, Jungwirth third and Wood fourth.

Some 10 million viewers watched the event on television.

What happened in space, some 500 miles above the earth, on 4 October 1957?

The first Russian-made satellite went into orbit

The satellite was called Sputnik I and took about 95 minutes to complete each orbit of the earth. Radio signals were picked up by the BBC and RCA in the United States as well as by many amateur radio enthusiasts. The satellite was about 22 inches (560 mm) in diameter and weighed 185 pounds (83.6 kilograms).

Queen Elizabeth II being crowned

This was the first coronation to be seen all over the world on television. Carrying the Queen to take the coronation oath at Westminster Abbey, the gold coach was pulled through the streets of London at a walking pace. The day, 2 June 1953, was both cold and wet.

There was a shortage of professional coachmen for the proceedings, but millionaires and business men dressed up as Buckingham Palace servants to drive British and foreign Prime Ministers.

At midnight, the Queen and the Duke of Edinburgh made a final appearance on the balcony of Buckingham Palace. A huge cheering crowd, still wild with excitement, released balloons and streamers and waved umbrellas and bowler hats. Hundreds of fireworks were released on the Victoria embankment.

High Noon (1952)

This western film was not only popular but also controversial. Frank Miller arrives on the noon-day train at Hadleyville station to be met by three cronies. All seek revenge on Marshall Will Kane (Gary Cooper), who had sent Miller to prison. It is Kane's wedding day. A haunting background is provided by Tex Ritter singing the ballad 'Do Not Forsake Me, O My Darling'. Grace Kelly plays the bride.

Many people thought the film was really about standing alone against the McCarthy threat. John Wayne made a later version of the story (*Rio Bravo*, 1959), in which the sheriff takes all the help he can get.

Joseph Stalin

Stalin was largely responsible for transforming Russia into the dominant republic of the USSR. He had ruled Russia with an iron fist for almost 30 years. He died from a brain haemorrhage on 5 March 1953.

In his later years, he became increasingly paranoid. This was reflected in new surges of repression. Yet, when he died, people wept in the streets.

Stalin was one of the most successful tyrants in history and responsible for more deaths than anyone in history, with the possible exceptions of Genghis Khan and Hitler. Only recently has Europe begun to free itself from his legacy.

In 1950, the 2,000-year-old body of a man was discovered in a peat bog in Denmark.

True

The body was found in a bog near Aarhus, in Jutland. It was a man, wearing a leather belt and a skull cap, who had been killed by hanging or garrotting with a braided leather rope. The body was remarkably well preserved in the peat. This enabled scientists to establish that he had eaten some 12 to 24 hours before he died, and had lived on a thin gruel of grain and wild plant seeds. He had three days' growth of stubble on his chin.

He became known as Tollund Man, after Tollund Mose, the name of the bog in which he was found.

In 1951, Humphrey Bogart and Katharine Hepburn starred in a film called The Arabian Queen.

False

They did make a film, but it was called *The African Queen*. The film won Bogart an Oscar for his performance in the 1952 Academy Awards. It was directed by John Huston, who was supposedly one of the few directors able to get a performance from the very casual Bogart.

Princess Elizabeth and the Duke of Edinburgh were on safari in Kenya when her father, King George VI, died and she became Queen.

True

They were staying at Treetops Hotel. The royal tour, which her father had been unable to make because of ill health, was discontinued. The Queen arrived back in England to be met by the Prime Minister, Winston Churchill, and the Opposition Leader, Clement Attlee.

PUZZLE 4 TRUE OR FALSE?

A Ford Popular car could be bought in 1953 for £390, including purchase tax.

True

A two-door version of Austin's A30 cost £475, including purchase tax. A four-door Standard Eight was £481, but Ford undercut both by bringing out a cut-price revival of the old Anglia, renamed the Popular, making it the cheapest of Britain's small family cars.

Smog masks could be obtained on prescription in 1953.

True

Doctors were able to prescribe masks for people living in smoky industrial areas if they suffered from heart or lung disease. There was a choice of two masks, both of which had refill pads of gauze and cotton. The masks cost one shilling and were considered a stop-gap until the Government took action to eliminate smog.

James Dean, the actor, died in an air crash on 30 September 1955.

False

James Dean died when his car, a Porsche Spider 550, collided with a Ford Sedan. He was killed instantly. The 23-year-old had made only three significant films: *East of Eden* (1954), *Rebel Without a Cause* (1955) and *Giant* (1956). He had, however, made numerous television dramas. Seldom has so large a reputation been built on so few films.

TRUE OR FALSE? PUZZLE 4

The 1956 Olympics were held in Sydney, Australia.

False

The games were held in Melbourne, Australia. Notable amongst the gold medal winners was Chris Brasher (3,000 metres steeple-chase) who was the first British track athlete to win an individual Olympic title in 24 years. Judith Grinham won the women's 100-metre backstroke and Margaret Edwards came third in the same event.

The number of the first premium bond £5,000 prize winner was chosen by ERIC on 1 June 1957.

False

The prize was drawn by ERNIE, formally known as the Electronic Random Number Indicator. The Prime Minister, Harold Macmillan, inaugurated the improved Bond scheme and set the process in motion for the first prize to be drawn. The lucky number was 2VL861801.

Britain's first stretch of motorway, an 8-mile Preston bypass in Lancashire, was opened by the Prime Minister, Harold Macmillan, on 5 December 1958.

True

After being driven along the motorway, the Prime Minister said it was 'a token of what was to follow' and it was 'the symbol of the opening of a new era of motor travel in the United Kingdom'. How true!

PUZZLE 4 *TRUE OR FALSE?*

By January 1959, two-thirds of the households in Britain had a television set.

True

According to the BBC, the number of people owning a television set was 24.5 million. They also watched it for about twelve-and-a-half hours each week. About 7.5 million viewers could receive BBC only. Despite this, nearly twice as many people watched ITV programmes rather than BBC.

Health warnings about smoking reduced the sales of cigarettes by 10 per cent in the late fifties.

False

In fact, the introduction of filter-tips may have boosted the sales of cigarettes. Sales of filter-tips rose from £10.1 million in 1957 to £18.2 million in 1958. This may have been influenced by statements linking lung cancer and smoking. Overall tobacco sales rose from £256 million to £260.8 million. Despite the health warning, trends may have been affected, but not sales.

Josephine and Daphne were the names of characters played by Tony Curtis and Jack Lemmon in the film Some Like it Hot *in 1959.*

True

In the film, the two men play jazz musicians who witness the St Valentine's Day Massacre and are seen by the mobster Spats Colombo (George Raft). In fear for their lives the two, disguised as women, sign up with an all-girl band.

The disguises work, but Joe (Tony Curtis) falls in love with the band's vocalist, Sugar Cane (Marilyn Monroe), who has a drink problem and also wants to marry a millionaire. How can Joe make advances to another woman when he is disguised as a woman himself?

During the film, Monroe gives her unique rendering of the song 'My Heart Belongs to Daddy'.

The Dam Busters (1955)

This film was a grimly realistic version of the heroic bombing raids on the Möhne and Eder dams in Germany's Ruhr valley during the Second World War. Wing Commander Guy Gibson, the pilot who led the mission, was played by Richard Todd and the inventor of the 'bouncing bomb', Dr Barnes Wallis, was played by Michael Redgrave. Eric Coates's stirring music for the film, 'The Dam Busters' March', soared high in the British hit parade.

Lord of the Flies (1954)

Lord of the Flies was William Golding's first novel and the book which made him famous. It is a gripping story which gives a Swiftian picture of how boys would behave if stranded, unsupervised, on a desert island. The choirboys, stranded on an island after an atomic war, revert to savagery under the leadership of Jack Merridew. The story presents a chilling allegory of the savagery lurking beneath the thin veneer of modern civilized life.

Golding's other novels published in the fifties were *The Inheritors* (1955) and *Pincher Martin* (1957).

The opening of Disneyland

Disneyland, California, opened to the public on 15 July 1955. It was the world's most elaborate amusement park. It cost 17 million dollars to build and featured attractions such as a drive in the car of the future, a ride on a Mississippi stern-wheeler and rocket trips to the moon. It expected to attract crowds of around five million a year.

Disneyland was founded in 1954 as a base for Walt Disney's television productions. It does not seem to have lost its appeal since then!

Ruth Ellis

In June 1955, Ruth Ellis was found guilty of murdering the man she loved. She shot David Blakely, a 24-year-old racing-car driver, outside a North London public house on 10 April 1955. At her trial, when asked what she had intended when she fired the Smith and Wesson, she said, "I intended to kill him."

The jurors were instructed that in English law jealousy was not a defence. The jury found her guilty in 14 minutes. Although strong petitions were organized, on 13 July 1955, Ruth Ellis became the last woman in Britain to be hanged. It was suggested that no reprieve was granted because a passer-by was wounded by one of the shots fired at Blakely.

PUZZLE 5 *WHAT'S THE CONNECTION?*

CAN YOU PUZZLE OUT THE CONNECTION BETWEEN THE FOLLOWING?

Prince Philip
Princess Elizabeth
Princess Anne
15 August 1950

Princess Anne was born

Princess Anne was the second child of the then Princess Elizabeth and Prince Philip. Her full name is Princess Anne Elizabeth Alice Louise. Prince Philip married Princess Elizabeth on 20 November 1947. He was born in Corfu, the son of Prince Andrew of Greece. In 1947, he also renounced his rights of succession to the Greek and Danish thrones and became a naturalized British subject, adopting the name Mountbatten.

Monte Bello Islands
Atomic weapons
October 1952

Britain's first atomic weapons were tested

Britain's first atomic weapons were successfully exploded in the Monte Bello Islands, off the north-west coast of Australia. The bombs had been attached to a tower on one of the islands for the test. Observers on the mainland 100 miles away saw the blast and felt a heavy air pressure pulse some 4 minutes and 15 seconds after the flash of the explosion.

Doris Day
Howard Keel
The Deadwood Stage

The film *Calamity Jane* (1953)

In the film, Doris Day played Calamity Jane and Howard Keel played Wild Bill Hickok. The story began with the buckskin-clad Doris Day on top of the Deadwood Stage, singing "Oh, the Deadwood Stage is a headin' on over the hills." Earlier Day films included *Tea for Two* (1950), *On Moonlight Bay* (1951) and *April in Paris* (1952). Doris Day's real name is Doris von Kappelhoff.

WHAT'S THE CONNECTION?

Never Say Die
2 June 1954

The Derby at Epsom

Lester Piggott, then 18 years old, rode Never Say Die and became the youngest jockey to win the Derby. He took the lead with a furlong to go and won by two lengths from Arabian Night. His horse was American-bred and was a 33–1 outsider. Two years earlier, when he was 16, Piggott had finished second.

Winston Churchill
Graham Sutherland
30 November 1954

A portrait of Churchill

On 30 November, Prime Minister Winston Churchill celebrated his birthday by receiving a portrait of himself from MPs at Westminster Hall. The portrait, painted by Graham Sutherland, was presented by Mr Attlee and showed Churchill seated, gripping the arms of his chair. Sutherland was known for doing unflattering pictures. On accepting the painting, Churchill showed his dislike by saying it was 'a remarkable example of modern art' and that 'it certainly combines force with candour'.

Churchill resigned the premiership in 1955 and was succeeded by Anthony Eden.

Le Mans
11 June 1955

Motor-car racing

Three cars travelling at about 150mph crashed and burst into the spectators' grandstand, killing 80 people and injuring over 100 others. The race, it was decided, should continue, but the winning drivers (Mercedes) gave up their titles after discovering one of their team cars was involved.

Toothpaste
Television
22 September 1955

The first advertisement shown on television

Commercial television began on 22 September with a variety show and drama linked by the actor Robert Morley. There were six minutes of adverts shown during the variety show, the first being for S.R. Toothpaste, showing a toothpaste tube and a toothbrush sticking out of a block of ice.

Humbert Humbert
A 'nymphet'
Vladimir Nabokov
A love story

The novel *Lolita* (1955)

Vladimir Nabokov was born in Russia but became an exile when his family was ruined by the revolution. After a time in Europe he became an American citizen, although he died in Switzerland.

Lolita was Nabokov's most famous book. It is the study of an obsession. A middle-aged man, Humbert Humbert, becomes infatuated to the point of madness with a 'nymphet' — his seductive stepdaughter. The book was thought outrageous by many and by others to be a tender, but perverted, love story. Incidentally, there is not an obscene term in the book.

Thousands of gallons of milk
October 1957

A radioactive leak

Following a fire, which involved the leak of massive amounts of radioactivity up the 500-foot chimney at Winscale, Cumberland, thousands of gallons of contaminated milk from surrounding farms were poured down drains. Sales of milk, from a land strip seven miles long and two miles wide, were banned.

The Atomic Energy Authority stated that most of the radioactivity had been carried out to sea by the wind and that there was no direct danger to the public. Nobody was injured in the fire, which had started when some fuel rods overheated.

WHAT'S THE CONNECTION?

Stockholm
Football
29 June 1958

Brazil won the World Cup

Brazil beat Sweden 5–2 in the World Cup final in Stockholm. Brazil were at their best and the team included Garrincha and a 17-year-old, Pele.

Buddy Holly
Richie Valens
J.P. (Big Bopper) Richardson
3 February 1959

A plane crash

Buddy Holly and his two rock star friends died in a plane crash near Mason City, Iowa. They were on their way to perform in a show in North Dakota. Holly, who was 22, had toured Britain in 1958 with the 'Crickets'. His songs included 'That'll be the Day', 'Blue Suede Shoes' and 'Rave On'. Valens also had a hit with 'Donna' and the Big Bopper with 'Chantilly Lace'.

Holly was the first pop star to compose most of his own hits and arrange them as well. He also pioneered a new sound — guitars and drums without brass.

Dame Margot Fonteyn
A Panama City jail
April 1959
Prince Philip

An attempted coup

Dame Margot Fonteyn spent a day in a Panama City jail. She was accused of providing cover for her husband, Dr Roberto Arias, who was suspected of planning a coup, with Cuban help, to overthrow the government. The coup was supposedly timed to coincide with Prince Philip's making a one-day visit to Panama in the royal yacht *Britannia*. Dame Margot somehow persuaded the police that she knew nothing about the coup and was released.

Skiffle

Skiffle was alternative home-grown music in the fifties, before rock 'n roll. Youths gathered in coffee bars where steaming Gaggia machines dispersed frothy coffee, frequently served in glass cups. Cane furniture, rubber plants and a juke box normally provided atmosphere. Three-chord guitar players often sang folk music accompanied by a bass made out of a tea-chest and a broomhandle and a wash-board to provide rhythm.

Numbers such as Lonnie Donegan's 'Puttin' on the Style' and 'Rock Island Line' were popular.

Mount Everest conquered

On 29 May 1953, Sir Edmund Hillary (New Zealand) and Sherpa Tensing Norgay (Nepal) scaled Everest, at 29,028 feet the world's highest mountain. There had been nine previous attempts. This expedition approached the mountain from the south-west and established eight camps on the ascent. The climbers left the Union Jack, the Nepalese flag and the flag of the United Nations on the summit.

Billy Graham

The American evangelist, Billy Graham, led a three-month mission to the UK, which reached a climax on 22 May 1954. Reported attendances at his meeting were up to 1,300,000, with over 28,000 'conversions to Christ'.

Graham pioneered multi-media presentation of gospel preaching in the fifties and made television appearances world-wide. He also wrote a number of books, including *Peace With God* (1953) and *The Seven Deadly Sins* (1955). He came from a South American Baptist background.

Hancock's Half Hour

This was the fifties radio series for which Tony Hancock was best known. In it, he established the character of a doleful, opinionated nobody, with social pretensions, snobbery and prejudice against the ignorance all around him, for which he became so famous. Later, he made some films: *The Rebel* (1961), *Those Magnificent Men in their Flying Machines* (1965) and *The Wrong Box* (1966). He died in 1968.

FAMOUS PEOPLE CROSSWORD

DRAW THIS CROSSWORD ON A BLACKBOARD, PHOTOCOPY THIS PAGE AND GIVE IT TO EACH PERSON, OR USE THE CLUES AS A STRAIGHT QUIZ

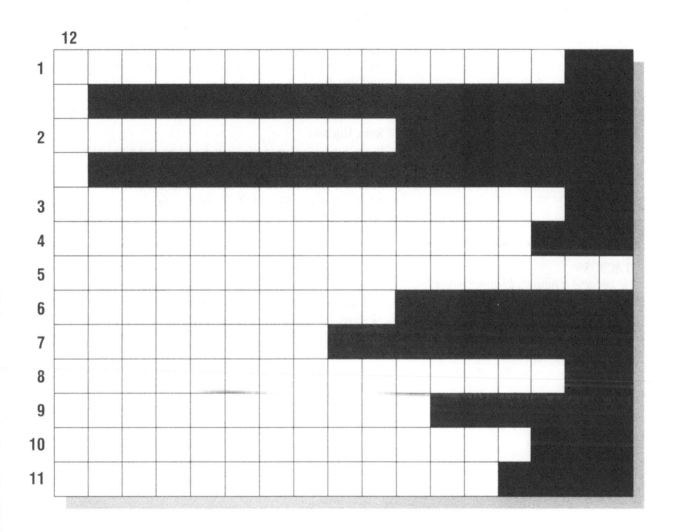

PUZZLE 6 *FAMOUS PEOPLE CROSSWORD*

1 ACROSS

A philosopher who campaigned against nuclear arms and won the Nobel Prize for Literature in 1950.

Bertrand Russell

Arguably the most influential and important philosopher of the century, Bertrand Russell was always controversial. He was imprisoned in 1914 for pacifist agitation — writing against conscription. In 1961, he was briefly imprisoned a second time for his opposition to nuclear weapons. His *History of Western Philosophy* (1945) was very successful and he won the Nobel Prize for his book *Marriage and Morals*.

2 ACROSS

He was 6' 4" tall and co-starred with Jane Wyman in the film, Magnificent Obsession *(1954).*

Rock Hudson

Rock Hudson became a fully fledged star at the age of 29 with this film. He played a drunken playboy who causes, and then cures, Jane Wyman's blindness. Other films he made in the fifties included *The Lawless Breed* (1952), *Back to God's Country* (1953) and *Pillow Talk* (1959).

3 ACROSS

He became a household name when he published The Alexandria Quartet, Justine *(1957),* Balthazar *(1958),* Mountolive *(1958) and* Clea *(1960).*

Lawrence Durrell

Lawrence Durrell was an English poet, humorous writer and novelist. He was born in India and lived abroad for most of his life. Although he wrote other novels, they were not as widely read as *The Alexandria Quartet*, on which his reputation as a novelist stands. The books appealed particularly to young people. Each one tells the same story, but from different points of view, and is based on the theory that nothing can be absolutely true. Some critics thought of Durrell as the poor man's Proust.

FAMOUS PEOPLE CROSSWORD PUZZLE 6

4 ACROSS
He died on 18 April 1955 and was best known for his General Theory of Relativity.

Albert Einstein

His theory was published in 1915, when Einstein was a 26-year-old civil servant in Berne. It began with a demonstration that the speed of light is constant in all situations. He decided that time is variable: there are no absolute markers for time, or for space; it all depends on the observer's viewpoint.

Einstein also revealed how much energy is locked up in the atom and urged the Allies to develop the atom bomb before Germany could. Later, he signed a plea for the renunciation of nuclear weapons. He lived in Princeton, New Jersey, and was 76 when he died.

5 ACROSS
An English novelist best known for his sea stories, one of which was called The Cruel Sea *(1951).*

Nicholas Monsarrat

The Cruel Sea was one of the most successful novels about the Second World War. It contained graphic descriptions of action. His other books included *The Tribe That Lost Its Head* (1956) and *The Story of Esther Costello* (1953).

Monsarrat was born in Liverpool and educated at Winchester and Trinity College, Cambridge, where he took a law degree. After two years in a law office he turned to a writing career. During the Second World War he served as a naval officer.

6 ACROSS
He was known as the 'King of Hollywood'. In 1953, he starred in a movie with Ava Gardner called Mogambo, *playing a white hunter and guide.*

Clark Gable

Mogambo was a remake of a film called *Red Dust*, in which Gable had also starred 20 years earlier with Jean Harlow and Mary Astor. He was probably best known for his role as Rhett Butler in *Gone With the Wind* (1939). He was married to Carole Lombard for a few years before she died in an air crash in 1942.

Gable died in 1961, 12 days after completing the film, *The Misfits*. He had a heart attack brought on, it was thought, by the action scenes he insisted on doing himself rather than use a stand-in.

PUZZLE 6 *FAMOUS PEOPLE CROSSWORD*

7 ACROSS
He played 'Shane' in the film of the same name in 1953.

Alan Ladd

Shane was Alan Ladd's most popular part. Shane is a buckskin-clad gunman who rides into a Wyoming valley and helps a homesteading family in their battles against the cattle farmers and their hired killer. He tries not to use his gun until he is forced to do so. The story is told from the viewpoint of the homesteaders' son. Jack Palance and Van Heflin also starred.

Being small, Alan Ladd suffered from 'sizeist' jokes all his career, but was successful partly because of his brooding, choirboy features that suggested violence. He died in 1964 at the age of 51. He said of himself: "I have the face of an ageing choirboy and the build of an under-aged featherweight."

8 ACROSS
He helped Blackpool win the FA Cup at Wembley in 1953 and was known as 'The wizard of dribble'.

Stanley Matthews

Blackpool won 4–3 against Bolton Wanderers. Stanley Matthews was the idol of soccer fans for over a quarter of a century. He won 54 caps for England but is best remembered for his sportsmanship. During 33 years as a player he never received a caution or demurred at the referee's decision. The crowds were fascinated by his ball control, his unique body swerve, sudden acceleration and accurate passes.

9 ACROSS
A rock and roll singer who had a hit in 1957 with 'Rock with the Caveman'.

Tommy Steele

Tommy Steele and his group emerged with a British version of the rock and roll phenomenon which previously had been dominated by American singers. Other notables of the period were Lonnie Donnegan, Marty Wilde, Cliff Richard and Billy Fury. Steele was discovered in a Soho basement coffee bar called 'The Two I's'. His real name was Tommy Hicks.

FAMOUS PEOPLE CROSSWORD **PUZZLE 6**

10 ACROSS
In 1955, he played 'Marty' in the film of the same name.

11 ACROSS
He was the centurion, Marcellus Gallilio, in the film, The Robe, *in 1953.*

12 DOWN
He was a circus acrobat before becoming an actor and starred in Trapeze *(1956) and* Gunfight at the OK Corral *(1957).*

Ernest Borgnine
This was a movie which touched hearts with its pure simplicity. It presented the love story between a Bronx butcher (Marty) and a girl who felt that her plain looks were working against her and who had been turned down on a blind date. Betsy Blair played the girl.

Borgnine won an Oscar for his role. He is probably best known for playing heavies, as in *From Here to Eternity* (1953) and *Bad Day at Black Rock* (1954).

Richard Burton
The Robe was the first Cinemascope film. Richard Burton has, at times, been more famous for his drinking bouts and his two marriages to Elizabeth Taylor than for his screen performances. *The Robe* also starred Jean Simmons and Victor Mature, who stole the acting honours as the slave Demetrius.

The robe was that worn by Christ, and for which a handful of Romans gambled. It was also a symbol of the conversion to Christianity of centurion Marcellus Gallilio. The role had originally been intended for Gregory Peck.

Burt Lancaster
Burt Lancaster was hard to categorize. He played many swashbuckling and tough-guy roles, but his talents were much broader. This was reflected in the variety of movies he made in the fifties: *Come Back Little Sheba* (1952), *From Here to Eternity* (1953), *The Rainmaker* (1956) and *Separate Tables* (1958). His roles ran the gamut from tough guys and cowboys to pirates, prophets and people from ethnic minorities. He certainly showed himself to be versatile.

the 1960s

THE SIXTIES, more than any decade before it, saw the pace of change speed up. Many older people felt that the world they lived in bore little resemblance to the way life had been before.

Technological advances made giant leaps, with the exploration of space and the development of surgery for heart replacement operations. The cold war seemed to be gathering momentum and in 1962, with the Cuban crisis, came very close to nuclear war. In Berlin, the newly erected Wall stood as a symbol of confrontational policies. Civil rights movements were fighting to be acknowledged. On television we saw man take his first steps on the moon surface. In the Middle East, the Israeli–Arab war broke out, once again pressurizing US–Soviet relationships. Computers were becoming familiar objects in industry and commercial enterprises.

Revolution seemed to be happening on all fronts — fashion, music, literature and the arts. Young people appeared to be rejecting all parental values. There was a boom in building housing estates. Former carpenters and painters reached tycoon status within a few years. Tradesmen and labourers were building a house every week and earning around £50 each. The working wife had become a feature of family life. Mass hysteria was commonplace at performances given by 'pop stars' such as 'The Beatles' and 'The Rolling Stones'. Permissiveness became a common word as sexual and social taboos were shaken by the contraceptive pill and the young taking drugs.

On the railways, steam locomotives were replaced by diesel engines. By 1965, there were few steam locomotives left. A tremendous increase in private car ownership meant fewer rail passengers, resulting in the closure of a large number of branch lines.

The rise in the quantity of consumer goods available meant more people with improved living standards. Holidays abroad, especially in Spain, were popular. By 1964, 36 per cent of British homes had refrigerators and 100,000 shops sold frozen goods, which had begun to be graded according to the length of time they could be kept fresh.

WHO DID WHAT? PUZZLE 1

NAME THE PERSON OR PERSONS INVOLVED IN THE FOLLOWING EVENTS

Who said, on 3 February 1960, "The wind of change is blowing through this continent and, whether we like it or not, this growth of national consciousness is a political fact"?

Harold Macmillan

He made the statement when addressing the South African Parliament in Capetown. He went on to urge the South African rulers to adopt policies of racial equality. The British Prime Minister was afterwards accused by white politicians of ignorant meddling.

Who shot down an American U-2 aircraft in May 1960?

The Russians

The Russians claimed that the aircraft, piloted by Francis Gary Powers, had deliberately violated Soviet air space on a spy mission, in order to wreck forthcoming Summit talks in Paris. The Americans countered that the pilot was carrying out weather research and had strayed off course.

The Summit, involving Eisenhower, Khrushchev, Macmillan and de Gaulle, which held hopes for improving East–West relationships, never got past its preliminary meeting. After three days of bitter recriminations, the Summit was abandoned.

Who became President of the United States of America on 20 January 1961?

John Fitzgerald Kennedy

John Kennedy, at the age of 43, became the youngest ever US President. He won the Presidency by one of the narrowest margins ever, to become the first Roman Catholic to be elected.

In his 10-minute inaugural speech, he said: "Ask not what your country can do for you — ask what you can do for your country."

PUZZLE 1 *WHO DID WHAT?*

Who became the first man to fly in space, on 12 April 1961?

Yuri Gagarin

His full name was Major Yuri Alexeyeritch Gagarin. He orbited the earth in a four-and-a-half-ton Vostok space ship, reaching a height of 190 miles, and returned safely after a flight which lasted 108 minutes. The space ship came back to earth using a parachute.

During the flight, Major Gagarin was strapped to a couch and did very little to fly the spacecraft. He mostly reported on what he could see and was monitored by instruments and cameras to record his responses to the stresses of the flight.

Who conquered the north face of the Eiger on 31 August 1962?

Chris Bonington and Ian Clough

Bonington was aged 27 and Clough 25 when they became the first Britons to conquer the north face of the Eiger. They made the ascent of the 13,040-foot peak in two days — one of the fastest ever.

Who told fellow MPs in a statement on 22 March 1963 that there was 'no impropriety whatever' in his relationship with Christine Keeler?

John Profumo

Later, in June, John Profumo, who was Secretary of State for War, resigned from the government and admitted that he had lied when he made the statement. A key figure in the affair was Dr Stephen Ward, a West End osteopath, who wrote privately to both the Prime Minister and the leader of the Opposition (Harold Wilson) informing them that Profumo met Keeler at his flat.

Keeler was said to be also having a liaison with a Soviet naval attaché. Another prominent figure in the scandal was Mandy Rice-Davis, who was Ward's mistress and Keeler's flatmate.

Which rag-and-bone men topped the TV ratings in 1964?

Steptoe and Son

This comedy series was about a family rag-and-bone business. It was claimed that 26 million viewers tuned in to watch the show. The central characters were Alfred Steptoe (Wilfred Bramble) and his son, Harold Steptoe (Harry H. Corbett). The series was written by Ray Galton and Alan Simpson.

Who won an Oscar in Hollywood for her role in the film, Mary Poppins, *on 6 April 1965?*

Julie Andrews

The Academy Awards ceremony in 1965 was dominated by British success. *Mary Poppins* won five Oscars and *My Fair Lady*, starring Rex Harrison, won eight, including best film of the year. The MC for the occasion, Bob Hope, remarked during the proceedings: "Welcome to Santa Monica on the Thames."

Julie Andrews went on to other successes, notably *The Sound of Music* (1965), which also won a best picture Oscar. Later, she tried to cast off her squeaky-clean image and create a sexual image for herself, but without success.

Who was charged with the 'Moors murders' in October 1965?

Ian Brady and Myra Hindley

Both Brady and Hindley received life sentences for the murders of two children — one 10 years old and the other 12 — whose bodies were buried on the moors, north of Manchester. Brady was also convicted of the murder of a 17-year-old youth, Edward Evans.

Brady and Hindley worked in the same office and had developed an appetite for sadism. Hindley's brother-in-law, David Smith — himself then 17 years old — witnessed the murder of Evans and then alerted the police.

PUZZLE 1 *WHO DID WHAT?*

Who succeeded Jo Grimond as leader of the Liberal party on 18 January 1967?

Jeremy Thorpe

Thorpe was elected Liberal MP for North Devon in 1959. After Jo Grimond stood down there was a hurried ballot of the 12 Liberal MPs to elect Thorpe as leader. At the time, many constituency Liberals felt 'undemocratically' bounced into accepting the new leader.

Which round-the-world yachtsman returned to his Portsmouth home on 4 July 1968 after sailing around the world?

Alec Rose

He returned to a massive celebration in Portsmouth. Some 250,000 people cheered him from the quayside. The trip around the world took him 354 days. Alec Rose, a greengrocer, was 59 when he made the journey in his small ketch, *Lively Lady*.

Who became the first man to step on the moon's surface on 21 July 1969?

Neil Armstrong

Watched by millions of television viewers, the commander of Apollo II climbed down a ladder from the lunar module Eagle and stepped onto the moon. His words were: "That's one small step for a man, one giant step for mankind." He was joined soon afterwards by fellow astronaut Edwin 'Buzz' Aldrin. The two men collected samples of dust and rock and left the American flag on the surface of the moon before returning to earth.

Fashions

By 1961, 'winkle-pickers' — narrow shoes with long, sharp toes — were in fashion. In 1962, the 'Beatle Suit' in black, with a round-neck, collarless coat, was worn by youths. This then gave way to loose tops with tight trousers or jeans.

Toddlers began to wear long trousers as soon as they could walk. Shorts for children became a rarity. Women's skirts became extremely short and the 'mini-skirt' made its appearance. Hemlines six to eight inches above the knee were common — many of the skirts skin-tight as well. Long leather boots often formed part of the outfit, but mostly stiletto-heeled shoes were worn.

High hairstyles were fashionable. By 1967, there was a floral cult. Flower-patterned dresses, tinkling bells on chains around the neck and long, flowing hair were 'in'. Both sexes frequently wore complete trouser suits in floral styles with flowers in their hair. Many young men emulated women by back-combing, bleaching and dyeing their hair.

Cosmetic surgery began to be popular. Surgeons, who had advanced their skills repairing faces shattered by war, now applied them to combat ageing. An average face-lift cost up to £300 in 1968. Other beauty aids of the period included hair pieces costing about £30 and false fingernails and eye-lashes.

The fuss over *Lady Chatterley's Lover*

The novel, written by D.H. Lawrence and published by Penguin Books, had been banned for 30 years and was the subject of a prosecution as a test case in 1960. On 2 November 1960, after a six-day hearing, cheers and applause broke out in the Old Bailey courtroom when the jury ruled that the novel was not obscene.

Penguin Books had some 200,000 copies ready to distribute after the hearing, at a cost of 3s 6d each. The prosecution at one stage asked the jury: "Is it a book you would wish your wife or your servant to read?" The answer was "Yes".

CAN YOU LINK THE PERSON NAMED WITH THE BOOK, FILM, MUSIC, SPORT OR SUBJECT?

Anthony Perkins	Cricket
Terry Downes	To Kill a Mockingbird
Joseph Heller	Football
Benjamin Britten	'She Loves You'
The Beatles	Psycho
Sean Connery	Boxing
Mary Quant	'We Love You'
Bobby Moore	Catch 22
Twiggy	'War Requiem'
The Rolling Stones	Dr No
Fred Truman	Fashion designer
Harper Lee	Fashion model

Anthony Perkins

Psycho (1960)

Anthony Perkins played Norman Bates who owns the motel in which most of the action in this film takes place. From the moment the victim, Marion Crane (Janet Leigh), checks in at the motel, feelings of foreboding are aroused. The killing in the motel shower is mainly left to the audience's imagination. Anthony Perkins was not even there when the sequence was shot — he was rehearsing another part on Broadway.

The character Norman Bates, created by Perkins, has lived on in the minds of movie-goers, as does the shower scene and Bates getting rid of the body in Crane's own car boot in a swamp.

Terry Downes

Boxing

Terry Downes became world middleweight champion when he defeated Paul Pender in the ninth round at Wembley on 11 July 1961. The defender sat down in the ninth round and said he had had enough. With the victory, Terry Downes became the British successor to Randolph Turpin, who won the same title ten years earlier.

Joseph Heller

Catch 22 (1961)

Catch 22, written by Joseph Heller, became the year's most talked about novel in 1961. It was a black comedy and stridently anti-war. The hero of the book, Captain Yossarin, decides that he cannot face any more bombing missions. His determination to stay alive, by feigning insanity to get out of flying the missions, proves to the authorities that he is sane enough to fly them — this is, in fact, Catch 22.

Other books written by Joseph Heller are Something Happened (1974) and Good as Gold (1979).

Benjamin Britten

'War Requiem'

The first performance of 'War Requiem' was in 1962, in the newly completed Coventry Cathedral. Benjamin Britten occupies an important place in European music. As well as being a pianist and conductor, he composed operas, music for film and radio, piano and violin concertos and a cello symphony, works for voice and orchestra and string quartets. He died in 1976.

The Beatles

'She Loves You' (1963)

Beatlemania was in full swing in 1963 when sales of 'She Loves You' passed one million to win the Beatles a gold disc. It stayed a number-one hit for four weeks.

The Beatles, George Harrison, Paul McCartney, John Lennon and Ringo Starr, reigned supreme through the sixties. Between1963 and 1969, they had an incredible 17 UK number-one hits. And in America, on 4 April 1964, they held all top five places on the singles chart with 'Can't Buy Me Love', 'Twist and Shout', 'She Loves You', 'I Want To Hold Your Hand' and 'Please, Please Me'. Their album 'Sergeant Pepper's Lonely Hearts Club Band', released in 1967, is the most coveted recording released by a rock group.

Sean Connery

Dr No (1962)

Sean Connery played James Bond in this thriller about an agent code-named 007 — licensed to kill. The film took time to find an audience, but was quickly followed by other films from the books about James Bond, written by Ian Fleming.

Bond is always sent by his boss, 'M', to do battle with the KGB or SMERSH and defeat villains with names like Dr No or Goldfinger.

SCRAMBLE PUZZLE 2

Mary Quant

Fashion designer

Mary Quant broke away from the restrictions of couture and created popular styles which became symbolic of the sixties. She opened her first shop, 'Bazaar', in the Kings Road in 1955. She designed clothes for young women who no longer wanted to wear what their mothers found acceptable.

Bobby Moore

Football

Captained by Bobby Moore and managed by Alf Ramsay, England beat Germany 4–2 on 30 July 1966 to win the World Cup. Moore made 108 appearances for England in full internationals between 1962 and 1974.

Twiggy

Fashion model

Twiggy, in 1966, was a 17-year-old fashion model who was rising to fame. She was a Cockney, weighed about six and a half stone, had huge eyes and waif-like looks. In 1966, she was said to be earning ten guineas (£10 10s) an hour working as a model.

The Rolling Stones

'We Love You' (1967)

The Rolling Stones achieved success in 1963 with the release of their first single, a reworking of an obscure Chuck Berry song called 'Come On'. The Stones' truculent performing style was a contrast to the more wholesome approach of the Beatles. Mick Jagger and Keith Richards soon began writing their own material, which rivalled that of Lennon and McCartney.

Other Rolling Stones hits included 'Jumpin' Jack Flash', 'Honky Tonk Woman', 'I Can't Get No Satisfaction' and 'Dandelion'.

Fred Truman

Cricket

In 1964, at the Oval, Fred Truman became the first bowler to take 300 wickets in Test cricket. His final total was 307. He played for Yorkshire from 1949 to 1968 and in 67 Tests for England, during the period 1952–65.

He was a right-arm fast bowler and during most of his career formed an opening bowling partnership with J.B. Statham. The total of wickets taken by Fred in first-class cricket was 2,304. He was popularly known as 'Fiery' Fred.

Harper Lee

To Kill a Mockingbird (1960)

Harper Lee was an American novelist from Alabama. *To Kill a Mockingbird* gives an account of a small Alabama town as it is seen through the eyes of an eight-year-old girl. Her father is a lawyer who defends a black man wrongly accused of rape.

The novel won the Pulitzer Prize and became one of the best selling novels of all time.

National Service ending

The last 2,049 National Servicemen received their call-up papers on 31 December 1960. The scheme had begun in 1939 and the total number called up reached 5,300,000. The enlisted men usually did two weeks' basic training and then went on to other units, often to learn a basic trade. Since National Service ceased, the forces have relied entirely on voluntary recruitment.

'Ready, Steady, Go!'

The show, 'Ready, Steady, Go!' started on ITV in August 1963, around the time Beatlemania was rampant. Rock groups played live in front of audiences, dressed in whatever was the latest trend. It became Britain's most popular live music show.

Cathy McGowen, known as 'Queen of the Mods', was a favourite host on the show. Artistes who appeared included: The Rolling Stones, The Kinks, The Animals, Manfred Mann, Tina Turner and Stevie Wonder.

Enoch Powell

Enoch Powell became famous for his views on the dangers he envisaged with the immigration of black people. In April 1968, he triggered fierce controversy in a speech he made in Birmingham in which he said: "As I look ahead, I am filled with foreboding. Like the Roman, I see the River Tiber foaming with much blood." Also, he said that Britain must be 'mad, literally mad, as a nation' to allow 50,000 dependants of immigrants into the country each year.

Edward Heath, who was the Opposition and Tory party leader, considered the speech to be racist and inflammatory and sacked Powell from the shadow cabinet.

Pope Paul saying 'No' to birth control

530 million Catholics had waited hopefully for Pope Paul's decision, but on 29 July 1968 he refused to make any concessions: he declared that any form of artificial birth control was against the divine will. Anyone disobeying the Pope's decision risked the possibility of excommunication.

Unusually, there was a lot of public quibbling by the Church leaders about the decision. Many were disappointed by the ruling.

What happened at Le Bourget airport in France on 16 June 1961, involving Rudolf Nureyev?

He defected to the West

The dancer broke away from his ballet company (Kirov) at the airport and ran up to a group of French police, shouting: "Protect me, protect me!"

The company of ballet dancers were scheduled to fly from Paris to London to appear at Covent Garden. Nureyev was 21 at the time. Russian officials tried to change his mind but he decided to stay and was granted political asylum.

What happened in Berlin in August 1961?

The Berlin wall was built

On 13 August 1961, the Soviet zone of Berlin was sealed off by the Russians and the Berlin wall was built. It was intended to stop the increasing exodus of East Germans who were seeking a new life in the West. East German soldiers, armed with machine guns, guarded the wall. Some 50,000 East Germans who worked in West Berlin were not allowed through to go to work.

Many East Berliners tried to find loopholes and ways to cross to the West. Many of them died in the attempt.

What did Lieutenant-Colonel John H. Glenn do in Space in February 1962?

He was the first American to orbit the earth

In his Mercury capsule, called Friendship 7, John Glenn lifted off from Cape Canaveral and then five hours later splashed down in the Atlantic, after orbiting the earth three times.

The flight had been postponed ten times because of weather conditions. On his re-entry it was thought that the heat shields on Glenn's craft were loose and that his capsule would burn up. In the event, the shields remained in place and he returned safely.

WHAT HAPPENED? PUZZLE 3

What happened to Marilyn Monroe in a bungalow near Hollywood on 5 August 1962?

She was found dead

She was found lying naked, clutching a telephone receiver, by two doctors who had been alerted by her worried housekeeper. There was an empty bottle of Nembutal tablets on the bedside table. She was 36.

Her films included: *Gentlemen Prefer Blondes* (1953), *How To Marry A Millionaire* (1953), *The Seven Year Itch* (1955), *Some Like it Hot* (1959) and *The Misfits* (1961).

She married an aircraft worker at 16, baseball star Joe di Maggio in 1952 and playwright Arthur Miller in 1956. Her real name was Norma Jean Baker.

What happened after a report called 'Reshaping British Rail' was published in March 1963?

Savage cuts to the rail network

The report proposed closing 2,128 stations, cutting the rail network by a quarter, scrapping 8,000 coaches and axeing 67,700 jobs. The chairman of the British Railways Board, Dr Beeching, had been brought in from ICI by the government to increase efficiency. Later, on 3 March 1964, the government announced the mass closure of railway lines, despite protests from many MPs and the unions.

What happened in many British seaside resorts in the summer of 1964?

Gangs of Mods and Rockers clashed

In teenage rituals, gangs of Mods and Rockers, armed with sticks and bottles, clashed at a number of South Coast seaside resorts. In Brighton there were 76 arrests and in Margate two youths were stabbed and 51 arrested. Trouble also erupted at Southend, Bournemouth, Clacton and Hastings.

PUZZLE 3 *WHAT HAPPENED?*

What happened at Buckingham Palace involving the Beatles on 26 October 1965?

They received MBEs

All four Beatles arrived in a Rolls-Royce with their manager Brian Epstein. Hundreds of police were brought in to deal with crowds of teenage girls who screamed, shouted and waved banners. The inclusion of the Beatles on the honours list gave rise to some controversy.

What happened to an H bomb being carried by a B-52 bomber close to southern Spain in February 1966?

It fell off the bomber into the Atlantic

The bomb was found on the sea bed by a midget submarine on 7 April 1966. There was great concern in Spain and America that the missing bomb might leak radiation. After two months' search it was found on the sea bed and reported as intact. There was great relief all round.

What happened at Wormwood Scrubs concerning George Blake in October 1966?

He escaped

George Blake, who was serving a 42-year sentence for spying, escaped using a home-made rope ladder, strengthened by 10 pairs of size 13 knitting needles, to scale the outer wall of Wormwood Scrubs. A pink chrysanthemum was left outside as a clue to the identity of those who had helped him escape.

On 20 November 1966, it was reported that Blake had turned up in East Berlin. The event was something of a propaganda coup for Russia.

WHAT HAPPENED? PUZZLE 3

What happened involving Israel between 5 and 10 June 1967?

The six-day war

On 5 June 1967, the tension building up between Israel and the Arab states erupted into war. Israeli planes launched strikes against the Arabs, destroying 374 planes and taking control of the skies. Tank battles raged against Egypt and Jordan.

By the second day it was becoming clear that Israel was heading for victory. By 10 June, fighting ceased and Israel halted her forces 12 miles into Syria. Total war casualties were estimated to be at least 100,000 dead.

In the fighting, Israel killed 10 US sailors in a torpedo attack on the ship *Liberty*, having mistakenly identified it as Egyptian.

What happened in Groote Shuur Hospital, Cape Town, in December 1967, involving Professor Christian N. Barnard?

He performed the first human heart transplant

The operation was carried out by a team of 30 doctors and nurses. The patient, Louis Washkansky, was a 53 year-old grocer.

Barnard introduced open-heart surgery to South Africa and developed artificial heart valves. Barnard's second patient, Philip Blaiberg, lived for 594 days after his operation. Since then, many thousands of heart transplants have been done. Unfortunately, rheumatoid arthritis cut short Barnard's career.

What happened in Prague in August 1968?

It was invaded by Warsaw Pact armies

The invasion ended a period of liberalization and reform in Czechoslovakia, in which Alexander Dubcek began a 'socialist democratic revolution'. The Russians, aware of the impact of these changes taking place, sent in the Warsaw Pact armies to end it.

Resistance was futile against the 600,000-strong force and Dubcek was replaced by a new leader. Restrictions were placed on the press and the formation of any new parties was banned.

Ban-the-Bomb demonstrations

One of the biggest demonstrations took place in Trafalgar Square on 17 September 1961. Violent clashes ended with the arrest of over 800 people. Well known and respected people demonstrated, including Canon Collins, who was the chairman of the Campaign for Nuclear Disarmament, John Osborne, George Melly and Vanessa Redgrave.

Trafalgar Square was jammed with some 15,000 people. Around 3,000 police struggled to arrest demonstrators staging 'sit down' protests.

Young people in the sixties

In the sixties adolescents began to earn wages previously unheard of for young people. As a result, they became targets for sales campaigns. Many earned £10 a week or more, had no responsibilities and frequently spent it all on clothes, records, dances, coffee bars and a motor-cycle or a car. There was tremendous pressure to be 'with it' and not 'square'.

The teenage world of 'beat' — pop dance and music — was so different from what their parents had experienced that teenagers lived in a separate world from grown-ups. Even eating habits had changed: teenagers favoured Wimpy bars and snack bars rather than restaurants or cafes.

A new term, 'discotheque', came into fashion. Radio announcers who ran record programmes became known as 'disc jockeys'. The 'flower people' (hippies) emerged. They believed in love and peace and used the slogan 'Make love, not war'. They frequently went barefoot. 'Flower power' was another phrase often used. Flower people believed that violence, if met by the gift of a flower, could be turned aside. Many people gave up good jobs to join them.

There was previously unheard of freedom for the young, and strong stress on the needs of the young. All sorts of activities and opportunities became possible. Suddenly, there were a growing number of youth hostels and youth employment officers, a Youth Service Development Council, grants and advice available.

The first colour television service

The first British colour television service began on BBC2 on Saturday 2 December 1967. The lowest-priced 25" colour television set could be brought for £250. At that time, a basic farmworker's weekly wage was £11 11s.

TRUE OR FALSE? PUZZLE 4

On 9 November 1960, Robert Kennedy was elected President of the United States of America.

False

John F. Kennedy was elected as the 34th President of the United States on 9 November 1960. John Kennedy, for many, stood as the living embodiment of the 'new generation' of Americans. He had headed and won a vigorous campaign against Republican Richard Nixon. The campaign introduced the first televised debates between candidates. It was, however, a close-run thing. Kennedy was elected by only a 0.1 per cent majority of the popular vote.

When elected to the House of Commons in May 1961, Anthony Wedgwood Benn was banned from sitting in the house.

True

Anthony Wedgwood Benn, who had inherited his father's peerage and was otherwise known as Viscount Stansgate, was banned. Even though he had doubled his majority when elected, he was not allowed to sit in the Commons. The ruling that a peer cannot sit in the Commons was upheld and it was decided that he should remain ineligible until there was a law enabling him to renounce his peerage.

On 28 July 1961, the High Court quashed his election victory and appointed his defeated opponent as MP.

Jack Hawkins played T.E. Lawrence in the film, Lawrence of Arabia, *in 1962.*

False

The role was played by Peter O'Toole. Hawkins played General Allenby. Other well known names in the film were Alec Guinness, Anthony Quinn, Arthur Kennedy, Anthony Quayle and Omar Sharif.

It was Peter O'Toole's first starring part and it made him into a major star. The film took three years to make and cost $15 million. It was filmed in Jordan, where Lawrence fought in campaigns during the First World War.

PUZZLE 4 TRUE OR FALSE?

The Russian leader, Nikita Khrushchev, was on holiday when he was ousted from power in October 1964.

True

After ruling as Soviet leader for six years, Khrushchev was ousted from power while on holiday in his villa by the Black Sea. He was succeeded as Communist party leader by Leonid Brezhnev.

He was accused by the Politburo of wilfulness in his style of leadership, of pushing through a series of hastily prepared schemes and disrupting industry, agriculture and the party.

Khrushchev, a small, stout man who started out as a pipe fitter in a coal mine, brought many changes to the Soviet Union. He broke up many of the labour camps and modified the powers of the secret police. He even made an anti-Stalin speech in 1956, which threw the Communist party into turmoil.

Edward Heath succeeded Harold Macmillan as leader of the Conservative party in 1965.

False

When Harold Macmillan resigned through ill health, he was succeeded by the Earl of Home, who renounced his peerage when he became Prime Minister and leader of his party in October 1963. Sir Alec Douglas-Home resigned as leader after the Conservatives were defeated by the Labour party, in October 1964. Then Edward Heath became leader of the Conservatives in opposition.

Ian MacLeod, who was Leader of the Commons, and Enoch Powell, who was Minister of Health, were amongst ministers who were refusing to serve under Lord Home at the time.

An eagle called 'Goldie' caused traffic jams around Regent's Park in March 1965.

True

Thousands of people crowded into Regent's Park to see 'Goldie', who had escaped from London Zoo. The golden eagle was seven years old and hopped from tree to tree, now and then descending to eat food provided by the crowd.

TRUE OR FALSE? PUZZLE 4

The World Cup was stolen in March 1966 and later found by a dog.

True

The cup had been stolen from a stamp exhibition in Westminster Hall. A ransom demand was made to the Football Association for its return. It was found by a mongrel dog called 'Pickles' in a south London garden. The dog's owner, David Corbett, saw the dog tearing at an object wrapped in newspaper, and on investigation found the World Cup.

In March 1967, the RAF bombed an oil tanker located between Land's End and the Scilly Isles.

True

Sea Vixens, Buccaneers and Hunters dropped 48 incendiary bombs and 1,200 gallons of napalm on the remains of the oil-tanker, *Torrey Canyon*. Oil from the ship, which had become grounded on the Seven Stones reef, was fouling Cornish beaches. Over 100 miles of coastline was polluted by some of the 100,000 tons of oil carried by the vessel. The Prime Minister held a cabinet meeting and it was decided that to bomb and set fire to the oil was the only way to stop it spreading.

Francis Chichester, the 65-year-old yachtsman, sank on his way into Plymouth harbour in May 1967, after sailing round the world.

False

He made a triumphant return on his yacht, *Gipsy Moth IV*. Hundreds of craft met him after his 119 days at sea, sailing non-stop from Sydney, Australia. He was greeted by the Lord Mayor of Plymouth at a special reception. He also received messages of welcome from the Queen, Prince Philip and the Prime Minister, Harold Wilson. However, he did arrive in Plymouth 10 hours later than expected.

PUZZLE 4 *TRUE OR FALSE?*

Brian Epstein, the manager of the Beatles, drowned in his own swimming pool on 27 August 1967.

False

Brian Epstein was found dead when his butler broke into the locked bedroom of his house in Belgravia. He had taken an overdose of sleeping pills. Epstein, the former owner of a record shop, discovered and then managed the Beatles. John Lennon said, "I do not know where we would have been without Brian."

London Bridge was sold to an Arab millionaire for £1 million in 1968.

False

London Bridge was sold to an American millionaire for £1 million. Each stone was numbered when it was dismantled, so that it could be reassembled at Lake Havasu, California, USA. The bridge erected over the Thames was designed by John Rennie. A new bridge was completed in 1973 which was 105 feet wide and carried six traffic lanes to replace Rennie's structure.

In July 1969, Senator Edward Kennedy was given a two-month suspended jail sentence for leaving the scene of an accident.

True

Senator Kennedy received the sentence for leaving the scene of an accident in which a woman passenger in his car was drowned. Mary Jo Kopechne, aged 27, died when the car plunged over a bridge on Chappaquidick Island, Massachusetts.

Mystery surrounded the gap of some eight hours between the time of the accident and Kennedy's reporting it. Miss Kopechne had been a secretary to the senator's brother, Robert, who was assassinated in 1968.

David Frost

The sixties was a popular time for David Frost on television screens. The programmes he was involved with included 'That Was The Week That Was', 'Not So Much A Programme, More A Way Of Life', 'The Frost Report', 'The Frost Programme', 'Frost Over England' and 'Frost on Friday, Saturday'. He also hosted the Apollo moon programme.

'That Was The Week That Was' was taken off the air earlier in 1964 than planned because of the general election. Politicians did not like its brand of criticism and some BBC governors thought that the programme was an embarrassment. Not so the public: it had an audience of over 12 million.

Dr Zhivago

This 1965 film of Boris Pasternak's Nobel Prize winning novel was set at the time of the Russian revolution. Omar Sharif played Dr Zhivago, a young idealistic physician whose love for his wife (Geraldine Chaplin) and the beautiful Lara (Julie Christie) is engulfed by the tide of history.

The movie took nine months to film in the frozen wastes of Finland and in Spain, where a giant set depicting Moscow in 1917 was built. Co-starring were Rod Steiger, Tom Courtenay, Alec Guinness and Ralph Richardson.

The 'I'm backing Britain' campaign

In January 1968, against a gloomy economic climate, five typists employed at Colt Heating and Ventilation Ltd, Surbiton, Surrey, stated "I'm backing Britain" by promising to work an extra half hour every day without pay, as a way of improving the situation.

Politicians and many personalities in the public eye praised the women. It was suggested that if everyone adopted this attitude Britain would become great again. Many politicians and personalities, such as Bruce Forsyth, cashed in on the optimistic notion and adopted the slogan. Posters, T-shirts, shorts and shopping bags appeared with Union Jacks on them, stating: 'I'm backing Britain'.

CAN YOU PUZZLE OUT THE CONNECTION BETWEEN THE FOLLOWING?

Albert Finney
Shirley Ann Field
Alan Sillitoe
A bicycle factory

The film *Saturday Night and Sunday Morning* (1960)

Albert Finney played the lead character, Arthur Seaton, in this film from a novel written by Alan Sillitoe. Arthur, an angry young man, works in a bicycle factory. In the film he says: "No sense working every minute God sends. I could get through it in half the time but they'd only slash me wages, so they can get stuffed. Don't let the bastards grind you down. That's one you learn. What I'm out for is a good time. All the rest is propaganda."

Arthur lives for the weekends when he can go fishing, go to the boozer and have it off with his workmate's wife. However, his real love is Doreen, played by Shirley Ann Field, but she is old-fashioned and wants a ring on her finger first.

'Sharks'
'Jets'
Maria
New York
Leonard Bernstein

The film *West Side Story* (1961)

'Sharks' and 'Jets' are the rival gangs in this 1961 musical, set in New York. Leonard Bernstein wrote the music. Riff (Russ Tamblyn) is the leader of the Jets and Bernardo (George Chakiris) leads the Puerto Rican gang called the Sharks. Natalie Wood plays Maria, Bernardo's sister, who is to marry a Shark, but meets and falls in love with a Jet — Riff's best friend. Songs from the film include 'Maria', 'Something's Coming', 'America', 'I feel Pretty', 'Gee, Officer Krupke!' and 'Somewhere'.

Eleven old age pensioners
Berlin wall
May 1962

They escaped from East Berlin

Eleven elderly East Berliners, seven men and four women, dug a tunnel underneath the Berlin wall. The tunnel was six foot high and took two weeks to dig out. When asked why they dug the tunnel so high the leader, a man of 81, said: "We did not want our wives to crawl, but to walk unbowed to freedom."

A missile base
America
Russia
October 1962

The Cuban missile crisis

In October 1962, America and Russia came close to nuclear war over the Russian missiles based on Cuba. The outcome was that Nikita Khrushchev promised that the Russian missiles would be dismantled and shipped back to the Soviet Union. In return, President John Kennedy promised that the United States would not invade Cuba and would lift the blockade imposed on Cuba by the USA.

£2.5 million
British Rail
8 August 1963

The Great Train Robbery

On 8 August 1963, some £2.5 million was stolen when an armed gang held up an overnight Royal Mail train travelling from Glasgow to London. The robbery took place at 3.10am, near Linslade in Buckinghamshire.

15 raiders used four six-volt batteries to simulate a red stop signal. They coshed the driver, Jack Mills, uncoupled the engine and some of the carriages, and drove them further along the line to Bridego Bridge. They then loaded the mail bags onto a waiting lorry.

Charlie Wilson, the first Great Train Robber to stand trial, was arrested later in August.

John F. Kennedy
Lee Harvey Oswald
22 November 1963

The assassination of John F. Kennedy

John Kennedy was shot by Lee Harvey Oswald in Dallas, Texas, on 22 November 1963. The shooting happened as the presidential motorcade drove through the city's main business centre. Oswald fired three shots from the sixth floor of a nearby building. The President slumped forward, hit in the head and neck. Mrs Kennedy cradled her husband's head as the car sped to the Parklands Hospital, where the President died without regaining consciousness.

Lee Harvey Oswald, a 24-year-old former marine, was arrested within a few hours and charged with murder.

Jack Ruby
An underground car park
24 November 1963

Jack Ruby shot Lee Harvey Oswald

Lee Harvey Oswald was shot at point-blank range by Jack Ruby in an underground car park in Dallas. He was being transferred from police headquarters to the county jail. Oswald died without confessing that he had killed the President.

Jack Ruby was the 52-year-old owner of a Dallas striptease club. He was quoted as saying: "I did it for Jackie Kennedy." However, there was speculation that he was a co-conspirator and did it to silence Oswald. Later, in September 1964, the Warren Commission Report on the assassinations concluded that both men had acted on their own initiative.

Ian Smith
Rhodesia
11 November 1965

Ian Smith declared Rhodesia an independent state

A few days after the Prime Minister, Harold Wilson, held talks with the Rhodesian Prime Minister, the latter unilaterally declared Rhodesia independent. The British responded immediately by rushing emergency legislation through Parliament to impose sanctions against Ian Smith's action.

Incomes policy
Raging inflation
Harold Wilson
20 July 1966

A pay freeze

Faced with continuing high inflation, the Prime Minister, Harold Wilson, announced a six-month freeze on wages and dividends. Other measures included prices frozen for 12 months, no increases in purchase tax and hire-purchase limitations.

WHAT'S THE CONNECTION? PUZZLE 5

Dr Emil Savundra
Fire, Auto and Marine Insurance Co
£1.4 million

Fraud

Dr Savundra was the chairman of Fire, Auto and Marine Insurance Co, which collapsed in 1966 with losses estimated at £1.4 million. Dr Savundra was arrested on 10 February 1967 — a few days after being interviewed on television by David Frost — and charged with fraud. Savundra, on meeting some of the people who had been victims of the fraud during the interview with Frost, said: "I do not want to cross swords with the peasants."

Ambassador Hotel, Los Angeles
Senator Robert Kennedy
5 June 1968

Robert Kennedy was assassinated

The senator, who was the brother of John F. Kennedy, had been making a speech, after his success in the California primary elections for the Democratic Presidential nomination, when he was shot in the head and shoulder. His assassin, Sirhan Bishara Sirhan, a Jordanian Arab, was arrested immediately. Kennedy was rushed to hospital but died 24 hours later without regaining consciousness. He was 42.

Muriel Spark
Maggie Smith
Jean Brodie
Edinburgh

The film *The Prime of Miss Jean Brodie* (1969)

Muriel Spark wrote the novel, which became a play and then a movie. The film starred Maggie Smith as Jean Brodie. It was about an Edinburgh schoolmistress in the 1930s, whose influence on her class of girls becomes an increasing concern to the school. Celia Johnson played the headmistress, Miss Mackay, who becomes Miss Brodie's adversary.

DO YOU REMEMBER?

The changes in women's roles

The working wife had become a feature of family life in the sixties. This meant a change in the way home tasks were carried out. Chores formerly done by the housewife had to be shared by husbands in the evenings and at weekends. Many women found themselves doing a job and all the home chores — in effect, two jobs. The organizing of meals was particularly demanding. Shopping became a necessary labour. All these demands produced stress and strain and the traditional family circle began to decline.

In the sixties, both husband and wife frequently needed to work to pay for a new house, new furniture, labour-saving devices and items such as washing machines, refrigerators and so on, which now verged on being essential to every household.

Young women from low-income families were no longer forced into domestic work. Many other opportunities drew them away from the kitchen sink. Women now became judges, doctors and cabinet ministers.

The changes in family life were largely due to the progress of women and their altered status in society. Instead of being sheltered, a woman now frequently took the role of protector and organizer.

'Cathy Come Home'

This controversial television play was repeated in January 1967, despite complaints from local authorities that it was 'full of blunders'. The play, portraying a young homeless couple, shocked the viewers and led to the establishment of the charity, 'Shelter'. The author of the play, Jeremy Sandford, said that 'Cathy' was based on a real girl.

The hard-up royal family

Prince Philip, on an American television programme on 9 November 1969, said that the royal family might have to leave Buckingham Palace in 1970 if they went into the red. He complained that the Queen's allowance of £475,000 a year was based on costs of 18 years before. He denied any question of bad housekeeping: "We sold off a small yacht and I may have to give up polo," he said. Hardship, indeed!

FAMOUS PEOPLE CROSSWORD

DRAW THIS CROSSWORD ON A BLACKBOARD, PHOTOCOPY THIS PAGE AND GIVE IT TO
EACH PERSON, OR USE THE CLUES AS A STRAIGHT QUIZ

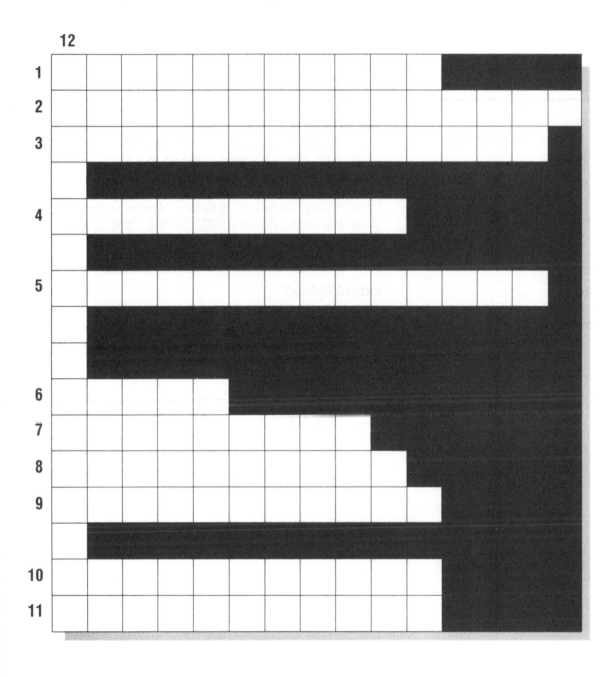

PUZZLE 6 *FAMOUS PEOPLE CROSSWORD*

1 ACROSS
The name taken by Cassius Clay when he became a Muslim.

Muhammed Ali
Cassius Clay won the light-heavyweight gold medal at the Rome Olympics in 1960 and then turned professional. He defeated Sonny Liston in February 1964 to become heavyweight champion of the world. His title was taken from him for refusing to join the US army. Later, he regained the title from Joe Frazier in 1974 and held it until 1978.

2 ACROSS
A portly, business-suited director of thriller movies.

Alfred Hitchcock
Alfred Hitchcock was a director who became as famous as the actors in his films. He started in movies as a junior technician in 1920, becoming a script writer, production manager and art director at Gainsborough Studios, Islington, by 1923. He became a director in 1925 and began making thrillers. Memorable films he made in the sixties were: *Psycho* (1960), *The Birds* (1963), *Marnie* (1964) and *Torn Curtain* (1966).

3 ACROSS
He was Jim Bowie in the film,
The Alamo *(1960).*

Richard Widmark
Richard Widmark started out in films playing villains, making his debut when he was 33. Previously he had been a teacher and a radio actor. Growing weary of being a villain, he began extending his range in *Broken Lance* (1954), *Time Limit* (1957) and *The Tunnel of Love* (1958).

The Alamo was the legendary story of 185 men who were massacred by the Mexican army on 6 March 1836. John Wayne played Davy Crockett, Laurence Harvey, Colonel Travis and Richard Boone, General Sam Houston.

FAMOUS PEOPLE CROSSWORD PUZZLE 6

4 ACROSS
He created James Bond.

Ian Fleming

The character Ian Fleming created — James Bond — became the best known fictional personality of his time. The books about Bond were attacked by some critics for dealing in 'sex, sadism and snobbery'. The Bond books published in the sixties were *Thunderball* (1961), *The Spy Who Loved Me* (1962), *On Her Majesty's Secret Service* (1963), *You Only Live Twice* (1964) and *The Man With The Golden Gun* (1965). Ian Fleming died of a heart attack on 12 August 1964.

5 ACROSS
He became President of America in 1963, after John F. Kennedy was assassinated.

Lyndon B. Johnson

He was sworn in as the 35th President of the USA within hours of the assassination of President Kennedy. The oath of office was taken in the Presidential aircraft with Mrs Jacqueline Kennedy by his side, her suit stained with her husband's blood. In 1964, Johnson stood as a candidate against Barry Goldwater and was then elected overwhelmingly to the office.

Johnson signed the Civil Rights Act in 1964, the most sweeping civil rights law in the history of the USA. He went on television and declared that the days of denying rights to negroes were over.

6 ACROSS
The silent Marx brother.

Harpo

Harpo — his real name was Adolph — performed in the family vaudeville act with his brothers Groucho (Julius), Chico (Leonard) and Zeppo (Herbert) from 1918. Once the brothers started making films, Harpo never spoke, but started miming instead. He made his harp, on which he was a virtuoso, his trademark. Harpo died on 28 September 1964, after a heart operation. He was 70.

PUZZLE 6 *FAMOUS PEOPLE CROSSWORD*

7 ACROSS
A singer who was known as France's 'Little Sparrow'.

Edith Piaf

Edith Piaf began her singing career in the streets and cafes when she was 15. She was only 4' 10" tall, but her voice brimmed with emotion as she sang of the tormented past. One of her most well known songs was 'Je Ne Regrette Rien'.

Piaf collapsed during the run of a show in 1961. She died in 1963. After hearing about her death, her friend and admirer, Jean Cocteau, had a heart attack and also died.

8 ACROSS
One of the gangland twins who terrorized the East End of London.

Ronald Kray

On 5 March 1969, both Ronald and Reginald Kray were given life sentences after being found guilty of murder. The judge said that they should not be released for 30 years. Another, elder brother, Charles, was also convicted of being an accessory. The trial lasted for 39 days.

9 ACROSS
He was Spartacus in the film of the same name.

Kirk Douglas

As well as playing the title role, Kirk Douglas was also executive producer for this epic story of a Thracian slave who led an army of gladiators in revolt against the tyranny of Rome in 73 BC.

Jean Simmons played the slave girl he fell in love with and Tony Curtis was his best friend. Other stars were Laurence Olivier, Charles Laughton and Peter Ustinov.

FAMOUS PEOPLE CROSSWORD PUZZLE 6

10 ACROSS
She married Robert Wagner and starred in the film Splendor in the Grass *(1961).*

Natalie Wood
Natalie Wood made her screen debut at the age of five, but never rose to the heights of Shirley Temple or Judy Garland. Later, she starred as Maria in *West Side Story* (1961). She played the notorious stripper, Gypsy Rose Lee, in the screen version of the 1959 hit musical, 'Gypsy' (1962) and Daisy Clover in *Inside Daisy Clover* (1965).

Natalie Wood was found drowned off Santa Catalina Island, California, on 29 November 1981. She was only 43, but had been a star for 38 years.

11 ACROSS
He was deputy leader of the Labour government led by Harold Wilson from 1964.

George Brown
George Brown had unsuccessfully run against Harold Wilson in 1963 to decide who would be leader of the Labour party after Hugh Gaitskell died. Together, as leader and deputy leader, they led the Labour party to electoral victory in October 1964.

George Brown earned himself a reputation for being volatile, truculent and emotional. In 1966, he became Foreign Secretary and was created a life peer in 1970. Later, he left the Labour party.

12 DOWN
In a speech given in Washington on 28 August 1963, during a Civil Rights march, he said: "I still have a dream. It is a dream chiefly rooted in the American Dream."

Martin Luther King
The words were spoken after 20,000 people marched through Washington to the Lincoln Memorial to press for Civil Rights. Amongst the crowd were celebrities like Marlon Brando, Burt Lancaster, Judy Garland and Bob Dylan

Dr King was shot dead on 4 April 1968 by an unknown white assassin. His last words to his friend, Reverend Jessie Jackson, were: "Be sure to sing 'Precious Lord' tonight, and sing it well."

On 7 June 1968, James Earl Ray was arrested in London for the murder.

the 1970s

AFTER THE effervescent sixties — swinging London and the permissive society — the seventies were very different. It was like the morning after, with unemployment, class and racial friction, economic slump and terrorism. Crises became a daily condition of life.

The heady bubble of idealism and the belief of young people that they could change the world — that science would unlock the secrets of the universe; that they could create a new kind of just, fair and equal society; and that, by dismantling all the repressive taboos and conventions of the past, individuals would be able to enjoy a greater degree of freedom and self-realization — burst. The dream, it turned out, produced a very different reality from that envisaged.

Astonishingly, Britain entered Europe. Flower power was out. There was growing violence in the world, muggings and burglary becoming commonplace. The rich got richer and the poor, poorer. America kept bombing Vietnam. The IRA stepped up its campaign of terror both in Northern Ireland and in Britain. War flared up again in the Middle East with the Yom Kippur war. The Palestinian problem fuelled international terrorism. Hijacks and hostages dominated the headlines.

Western nations slid into recession, oil prices rose sky-high and unemployment moved to the top of the political agenda. The discovery of North Sea oil, it appeared, would rescue Britain from a totally gloomy economic situation.

There were royal weddings, royal babies, royal silver weddings, the royal silver jubilee and the royal knockers, led by Willie Hamilton. There was a boom in Zen Buddhism, yoga and witchcraft. The fashion of 'streaking' gave way to more respectable jogging.

Calls for anti-discrimination laws were loud. Women, theoretically, achieved equality through the Equal Opportunities Act of 1975. Margaret Thatcher rose to power and 'Thatcherism' was born. In 1978, there were said to be 4.5 million people earning less than £55 a week, with plenty of those in catering, laundry work and clothes-making earning less than £44. At the end of the seventies, many people looked forward to the eighties with apprehension.

WHO DID WHAT? PUZZLE 1

NAME THE PERSON OR PERSONS INVOLVED IN THE FOLLOWING EVENTS

Who was elected Prime Minister on 19 June 1970, promising 'strong and honest government'?

Edward Heath

The election result was totally unexpected and against all poll indications. Nearly all opinions pointed to an easy Labour victory. In the event, Harold Wilson and his party had relied too heavily on the improved poll ratings brought about by large pay rises during the previous six months of his term of office, after a period of very tight controls.

During his period as Prime Minister (1970–74), Heath vigorously pursued entry into the European Community. He was also a gifted organist, conductor and yachtsman. In 1970, he won the Sydney to Hobart yacht race.

Who, on 3 June 1970, was the first British golfer to win the US Open Championship for 50 years?

Tony Jacklin

On winning the championship, Jacklin became the third golfer ever to hold the British and US Opens within the same 12 months. He won the British championship in July 1969.

To win, Jacklin beat the runner-up, Dave Hill (USA), by a margin of seven strokes. The previous British winner of the US Open Championship, 50 years earlier, was Ted Ray.

Which Australian tennis player beat Billie Jean King and then her own fellow countrywoman, Margaret Court, to win the women's singles title at Wimbledon on 2 July 1971?

Evonne Goolagong

Evonne Goolagong unexpectedly beat Billie Jean King in the semi-final and the reigning champion, Margaret Court, in the final — both in straight sets. Miss Goolagong, later known as Evonne Cawley, returned to England to win the championship again in 1980.

PUZZLE 1 *WHO DID WHAT?*

Which swimmer won seven gold medals at the Munich Olympics in September 1972?

Mark Spitz

This 22-year-old swimmer from California proved himself to be his sport's most successful competitor ever. He won all seven events in world record times — 100m and 200m freestyle and butterfly, 4 × 100m and 4 × 200m freestyle relay, and 4 × 100m medley relay. He also won two freestyle team golds at the 1968 Games, and between 1967 and 1972 set 27 world records for freestyle and butterfly events.

Which two American reporters uncovered the Watergate scandal in 1973?

Bob Woodward and Carl Bernstein

The two reporters worked for the *Washington Post*. After five burglars were caught putting listening devices on telephones in the Democratic party headquarters on 17 June 1972, the reporters discovered that a whole series of illegal and unethical acts had been carried out by the Nixon White House and Republican campaign for election. The affair ended with Nixon resigning as President of the United States.

Which member of the royal family was married on 14 November 1973?

Princess Anne

She married Captain Mark Phillips. He wore the scarlet and blue uniform designed for 1st The Queen's Dragoon Guards. Anne wore a Tudor-style wedding dress with a high collar and mediaeval sleeves. The full skirt was embroidered with silver and pearls. Both the bride and groom were world-class riders, she a European gold medallist and he an Olympic gold medallist.

WHO DID WHAT? PUZZLE 1

Which American heiress, previously abducted by revolutionaries, took part in a bank raid on 15 April 1974?

Patty Hearst

Patty Hearst, the 19-year-old daughter of millionaire publisher Randolph Hearst, was abducted from the apartment in which she lived in San Francisco on 4 February 1974. Ransom notes demanded that food be distributed to the poor of San Francisco.

On 15 April 1974, a hidden camera showed pictures of her with other bank robbers, armed and holding up a San Francisco bank. Later, she was arrested with other members of the Symbionese Liberation Army and was reported to have turned from being a hostage to a sympathizer.

On 20 March 1976, she was found guilty by a jury of assisting the bank robbers. The jury did not accept her story that she was brainwashed by her captors. She was jailed for seven years.

Who became leader of the Conservative party on 11 February 1975?

Margaret Thatcher

At the age of 49, Mrs Thatcher, the wife of a wealthy businessman and the mother of twins, became the first woman leader of a British political party. She won against four male rivals — William Whitelaw, Sir Geoffrey Howe, James Prior and John Peyton. She succeeded Edward Heath.

Who won the men's figure-skating gold medal at the Winter Olympic Games, Innsbruck, on 11 February 1976?

John Curry

John Curry became the first Briton to win a medal of any sort in the men's skating events. His early ambitions to be a ballet dancer — said to have been squashed by his father — influenced his style. His balletic grace, combined with athletic agility, gave him a decisive victory. He also won the men's figure-skating world championships on 4 March 1976. Later, in 1977, he founded the 'John Curry Theatre of Skating'.

PUZZLE 1 *WHO DID WHAT?*

Who launched his first cut-price 'skytrain' from Gatwick to New York in September 1977?

Freddie Laker

Against strong opposition from the major airlines, Freddie Laker launched his cheap flights. Some passengers queued for 24 hours to pay £59 for the first walk-on, no-frills, flights. Meals were offered for an extra £1.75. The normal fare charged by other airlines for flights to New York was about £186.

Although the airline establishment ganged up and eventually brought Freddie Laker down, he succeeded in breaking the cosy cartel of the anti-competitive aviation world that dominated air routes, and made them more competitive.

Who completed a 'hat trick' of men's singles titles at Wimbledon in July 1978?

Bjorn Borg

The 22-year-old Swede, who had an ice-cool temperament in crises, completed his 'hat trick' with a straight-sets victory over Jimmy Connors. No one had performed the feat since Fred Perry in 1934–6.

Who was announced as the 'fourth' man in the Burgess, Maclean and Philby affair to the House of Commons on 21 November 1979?

Anthony Blunt

A shocked House of Commons was told by Mrs Thatcher that the then Sir Anthony Blunt, art advisor to the Queen, was a spy for the Russians. Blunt, the Prime Minister said, admitted in 1964, after being granted immunity, that he had been a long-term Soviet agent. On the disclosure to the House of Commons, Blunt was immediately stripped of his knighthood by Buckingham Palace.

Princess Anne being named Sportswoman of the Year

In November 1971, Princess Anne was named Sportswoman of the year by the British Sportswriters Association. At 21, she was one of Britain's most accomplished all-round riders, and in September 1971, she won the European three-day event championship on her horse, Doublet.

The introduction of decimal coinage

After centuries of dealing in pounds, shillings and pence, suddenly, with entry into Europe, there was decimal coinage to cope with in 1971. Many people had difficulty understanding the new system. Also, the change seemed to have an inflationary effect.

It was goodbye to one-shilling pieces (5 new pence), the half-crown (12.5 pence), the florin (10 pence). And 'p' replaced 'd' for pence.

With the introduction of the new coins, a new attitude to money seemed to be born. Slogans such as 'Taking the Waiting Out of Waiting' began to appear, encouraging people to spend money they did not have. Credit cards — plastic money — were on the way in and money on the way out. People no longer saved up for something they wanted but arranged for a loan in some form instead.

Streaking

There was a frenzy of 'streaking' in the seventies. Naked people darted through streets and public buildings, and invaded the pitches at important sporting events. In March 1974, seven streakers sprinted across Kingston Bridge and were mentioned in *The Times*. One leapt the wickets at Lord's cricket ground and another ran around Twickenham rugby football ground. A 21-year-old woman, who was arrested, was reported in a paper to be a 'display artist'. One magistrate told another streaker: "You should be put in the stocks naked, so that people could throw stuff at you." A statement he probably regretted.

The skateboard craze

The seventies saw a giant epidemic of skateboarders. Streets seemed to surge with youths and children on wheels. Halls and parks were set aside for the use of youthful missiles in helmets, knee and elbow pads and gloves for protection. However, the craze appeared to subside almost as quickly as it arose.

PUZZLE 2 SCRAMBLE

CAN YOU LINK THE PERSON NAMED WITH THE BOOK, FILM, MUSIC, SPORT OR SUBJECT?

Richard Adams	Football
Gene Hackman	*The Towering Inferno*
Virginia Wade	Boxing
Gregory Peck	*Watership Down*
George Best	Tennis
Bobby Fischer	*The French Connection*
John Betjeman	*Shogun*
Pablo Picasso	Chess
James Clavell	*The Omen*
Robert Mitchum	Art
John Conteh	Poetry
Steve McQueen	*Ryan's Daughter*

Richard Adams

Watership Down (1972)

Richard Adams was originally a civil servant but scored a smash hit with his novel, *Watership Down*, in 1972. He writes allegorical nature/animal novels. His power as a writer lies in his ability to convey the way animals experience the world.

Watership Down is a tale about rabbits and appeals to both children and adults. His other works include *Shardak* (1974) about a bear, and *The Plague Dogs* (1977), a grim tale warning about the consequences of animal experimentation. Critics have alleged that he is 'politically reactionary' and 'sexist'.

Gene Hackman

The French Connection (1971)

This film was a semi-documentary thriller based on the exploits of real-life cop, Eddie Egan, and his attempts to track down an international drugs trafficker. Gene Hackman plays the cop — in the film he is called 'Popeye Doyle' — a self-righteous, obsessively driven man. Fernando Rey is the trafficking drugs boss.

The film is also known for its spectacular race between a car and a train on an elevated railway. The shooting of the sequence took six weeks. Gene Hackman won a best actor Oscar for his part in the film.

Virginia Wade

Tennis

Virginia Wade won the women's Wimbledon title in 1977, the year of the Wimbledon centenary and Queen Elizabeth II's silver Jubilee. She beat Chris Evert, the reigning champion, in the semi-final and Betty Stove in the final. Previously she had held the US title in 1968 and the Australian title in 1972.

Gregory Peck

The Omen (1976)

Gregory Peck starred in this movie as the US Ambassador to Great Britain who comes to believe that his adopted son is diabolically possessed. Lee Remick played Peck's wife. Other actors included Billie Whitelaw, David Warner and Leo McKern. The music, pounding satanically, was considered a masterpiece of its kind.

George Best

Football

In 1971, George Best, the Manchester United wayward genius, became one of the victims of the FA's determination to bring players' conduct into line with that expected on the continent. He was sent off for persistently arguing with the referee when United defeated Chelsea 3–2 at Stamford Bridge, on 18 August 1971.

Best played in 18 internationals over six seasons and won two championship medals with Manchester United, helping them to win the European cup.

Bobby Fischer

Chess

On 1 September 1972, the American, Bobby Fischer, beat the Russian, Boris Spassky, to become world chess champion. Fischer earned himself a reputation for being temperamental and unpunctual. He lived up to this by arriving an hour late for the award ceremony.

John Betjeman

Poetry

Sir John Betjeman became Poet Laureate in 1972. His poetry was usually traditional in form and outlook. When asked to become Poet Laureate, Betjeman said that he was 'dumbfounded'. "I thought there were better poets than me and they might be annoyed," he said. His work, however, was very popular.

Pablo Picasso

Art

The Spanish painter, Picasso, died at the age of 91 on 8 April 1973, from a heart attack. His output was phenomenal and has been estimated at 140,000 paintings and drawings, 100,000 engravings and 30 sculptures. Once, when looking at children's paintings, he said, "When I was their age I could draw like Raphael. It has taken me a lifetime to learn how to draw like them."

James Clavell

Shogun (1975)

The novel, *Shogun*, a long and detailed saga, is set in seventeenth-century Japan and was written by James Clavell. Australian-born Clavell was captured by the Japanese when he was 18 and imprisoned at the notorious Changi jail. His first book, *King Rat* (1962), is set in the jail and provides a study of relationships and characters of the prisoners in the face of cruelty and death. His second book, *Tai Pan* (1966), is about the founding of Hong Kong.

PUZZLE 2 SCRAMBLE

Robert Mitchum

Ryan's Daughter (1970)

Set against the background of the Irish troubles in 1916, this film tells the romantic story of an adulterous love affair between a village schoolmaster's wife (Sarah Miles) and a British officer (Christopher Jones). The schoolmaster was played by Robert Mitchum. Other stars included John Mills, Trevor Howard and Leo McKern.

The picture was filmed in Ireland, around the Dingle peninsula, County Kerry, and cost $6 million.

John Conteh

Boxing

John Conteh, from Liverpool, went 15 rounds at Wembley to become world light-heavyweight champion in 1974. He beat the Argentinian, Jorge Ahumada, on points. At 23, Conteh had 16 professional fights behind him. He became the first British holder of the title since Freddie Mills, 25 years earlier.

Steve McQueen

The Towering Inferno (1974)

Steve McQueen was the fire chief trying to bring the blazing highrise apartment block under control in this movie. There was no lack of supporting stars. They included Paul Newman, William Holden, Faye Dunaway, Richard Chamberlain, Jennifer Jones, Robert Wagner and Fred Astaire.

Fashions

The seventies brought a diversity and a lurching from one fashion to another. Shopkeepers did not know what to stock. 'Midi' and 'maxi' skirts took the place of the 'mini', with forays into 'hot pants'. Styles varied from the aggressively 'butch' to the 'coyly' sexy. Kaftans and 'ethnic' garb became popular. Many of these styles came from the Balkans, North Africa and the Middle East, and were frequently the cheap products of sweated labour.

Towards the end of the decade, fashions showed a marked masculine influence. Gone was gaiety, as was the traditional use of the word 'gay'. Some men were formal dressers, elegant in redis-covered suits, tailored shirts and ties. Others had beards and culti-vated a studious, tattered look. After mid-decade, male cosmetics took off in a big way. Male beauticians were giving facials and anti-perspirants began to sell in large quantities.

Bell-bottom trousers came and went. The punk craze brought an urge to look ugly. Punk rockers made themselves up with asex-ual ferocity. There were trash bags, T-shirts and safety pins through cheeks and nostrils. Fashion gave the impression of actors made up for a horror film. Eyebrows were plucked, lips were bright red, eyes and faces were smudged to look like ghosts or corpses. Leather was in and many wore storm-troop-like uniforms

The death of the Duke of Windsor

His Royal Highness, the Duke of Windsor, died at his home in the Bois de Boulogne on 28 May 1972. He was 77. Formerly Edward VIII, the Duke was the only British monarch to abdicate of his own free will. He had lived in self-imposed exile after giving up the throne in1936 to marry the woman he loved, Mrs Wallis Simpson.

According to the Duke's wishes for no state funeral, a simple private service was held in St George's Chapel in Windsor. The Duke's 75-year-old widow sat with the Queen and Prince Philip, screened off from the main congregation. The body was then interred in the royal family's burial ground at Frogmore, in Windsor Great Park.

What happened to England football captain, Bobby Moore, in May 1970 in Colombia, six days before he was due in Mexico to play for the World Cup?

He was accused of theft and imprisoned

The owner of a jewellery shop in a Bogota hotel accused him of stealing a bracelet. After being held for two days, he was provisionally freed. When he joined his team in Mexico he had to report regularly to Colombian officials and agree to attend the Columbian Embassy in London to hear the results of the case when he returned to Britain. The England team got through to the quarter-finals, which they lost to West Germany. Brazil won the cup. Later, after returning home, Moore's name was cleared.

What happened on the moon concerning David Scott and James Irwin on 31 July 1971?

They went for a drive

Using a Lunar Roving Vehicle (a 'moon buggy'), the two astronauts drove for several miles, while the third member of the crew, Alfred Worden, remained in orbit around the moon. The two astronauts became the seventh and eighth men to walk on the moon and the first to drive on it. The vehicle's front-wheel steering did not work, but they were able to manoeuvre with the rear wheels. Their spacecraft, Apollo 15, returned to earth safely, splashing down in the Pacific on 7 August 1971.

What happened at the headquarters of the 16th Parachute Brigade at Aldershot on 22 February 1972?

An IRA bomb exploded

The bomb was planted in a stolen car. It killed six civilians — four women domestic workers, a gardener and a priest — when it exploded. The IRA claimed the blast was in revenge for the death of 13 civilians in the previous month's 'Bloody Sunday' battle.

What happened in the Israeli Olympic compound near Munich on 5 September 1972?

'Black September' guerrillas took nine hostages and killed two others

The guerrillas demanded the release of 200 Palestinians held in Israeli jails, and a safe passage out of Germany. The Olympic Games were suspended and the West German Chancellor, Willy Brandt, took personal charge of negotiations with the terrorists. They were informed that they would be flown to an Arab country and were taken by helicopter to an airport 25 miles from Munich. As the terrorists walked to the waiting Boeing 727, just before midnight, German police sharpshooters opened fire. In the ensuing gun battle all nine hostages were tragically killed.

What happened in a chemical plant at Flixborough, Lincolnshire in June 1974?

The plant blew up

28 people were killed and hundreds injured. The factory was reduced to a charred metal skeleton after the blast. The force of the explosion devastated acres of surrounding farmland, some 2,000 houses were damaged and the village of Flixborough was evacuated as clouds of poisonous gas hung over the countryside.

What happened in the London underground at Moorgate on 28 February 1975?

A train crashed

The train rammed into the end of a dead-end tunnel, killing the driver and 34 passengers. The driver, instead of braking, appeared to have accelerated into the tunnel, ran out of track and crashed through sand piles and buffers. No satisfactory reason for the tragic event has been given. It remains a mystery.

PUZZLE 3 *WHAT HAPPENED?*

What happened in Vietnam in April 1975?

The last American troops withdrew

The war in Vietnam was over for America, and South Vietnam surrendered without a struggle to North Vietnam. The American evacuation ended with heart-rending scenes at the US Embassy as masses of Vietnamese swarmed around it. They were desperate to get on a shuttle service of helicopters taking people to safety on board warships in the South China seas. Marines used rifle butts to keep crowds back. On 10 April 1975, the last 11 marines were taken from the roof of the building by helicopter — the angry mob had opened fire, trapping them inside.

What happened on 4 July 1976 at Entebbe airport in Uganda, involving Israeli commandos?

They rescued over 100 hostages

An Air France A300-B Airbus had been hijacked after taking off from Athens airport on 27 June 1976 by a Palestinian group. They forced it to fly to Entebbe and demanded the release of 53 pro-Palestinian terrorists. Idi Amin, the Ugandan dictator, gave help to the skyjackers.

Before midnight on 4 July 1976, three Israeli transport planes landed, carrying 200 commandos. In 53 minutes they overpowered the Ugandan guards, killed seven terrorists, got the hostages aboard the transport planes and set off back to Israel.

What happened at Graceland, the Memphis, Tennessee mansion where Elvis Presley lived, on 16 August 1977?

He died

Elvis had been, for more than 20 years, the 'king' of rock and roll. He was 42 when he died. Things had never been the same for him after he came out of the army in March 1960. His manager, Colonel Parker, forced him to make third-rate 'beach movies'. In the seventies, Elvis spent most of his time reliving past glories in Las Vegas, or holed up in Graceland. He was the victim of terrible drug abuse — tranquillizers and barbiturates. John Lennon was reported to have said, "Elvis died the day he went into the army."

WHAT HAPPENED? PUZZLE 3

What happened to Charlie Chaplin's coffin in Switzerland on 2 March 1978?

It was stolen

Grave-robbers took the body from the cemetery, where he had been buried three months earlier. It was thought that a ransom was the motive, but no demands were left. There were marks on the ground showing that the coffin had been dragged before being loaded on a truck. The coffin was found in May 1978, buried some 10 miles from the original grave. Charlie Chaplin died on Christmas Day, 1977.

What happened when Argentina hosted the World Cup tournament in June 1978?

They won it

Argentina won a triumphant 3–1 victory over Holland. The Scots, who had high hopes under the management of Ally MacLeod, had a nightmare tournament. They missed a penalty and lost to the Peruvians. Winger Willie Johnson was sent home after admitting taking 'pep pills'.

What happened in the village of Mullaghmore, County Sligo, Ireland, on 27 August 1979?

Earl Mountbatten was murdered

It had been the custom of the Earl of Mountbatten for more than 30 years to spend August in this quiet village. He was well liked and had never felt the need of bodyguards.

He and members of his family set out for a day's fishing on their 30-foot boat, *Shadow V*. As the boat left the harbour, it was ripped apart by an IRA bomb. The Earl's grandson, Nicholas — who was 14 years old — and a 17-year-old boatman, died instantly. His daughter, her son Timothy and the Dowager Lady Brabourne were all seriously injured. Lady Brabourne died on 28 August 1979 from her injuries. The boat had been blown up by remote control.

The fuss over Dr Spock

In January 1974, Dr Spock's bestselling book, *The Common Sense Book of Baby and Childcare*, which had been the 'Bible' for millions of British and American families, was blamed for contemporary youth rebellion. Since the publication of his book in 1946, families had been following his advice to relax traditional controls and allow children to have their own way. The 'permissive society' apparently was all Dr Spock's fault. He denied the accusation and said that people had misinterpreted his original theory.

The Sex Pistols on ITV's 'Today' show

In December 1976, the notorious rock band, The Sex Pistols, appeared on the show and ran riot, resulting in the presenter, Bill Grundy, being suspended and EMI sacking the band. The group had a reputation for physical and verbal excess and had appeared on the show to talk about punk rock.

One of the band's members used an obscenity which Grundy asked him to repeat. After this, the interview quickly spiralled out of control. Grundy called them 'a foul-mouthed set of yobs'. Their manager, Malcolm McLaren, agreed and said they were proud of it.

The coronation silver jubilee

On the evening of 7 June 1977, her Majesty Queen Elizabeth started the festivities by lighting a giant bonfire in Windsor Great Park. This was the signal for lord lieutenants, mayors and bishops to light other bonfires from Land's End to Saxavord in the Shetlands.

The Queen and Prince Philip had been to a service of thanksgiving during the day at St Paul's Cathedral, followed by a banquet at the Guildhall and then a city walkabout. Street parties were held country-wide.

Mother Teresa

Mother Teresa was the founder, in Calcutta in 1948, of the Order of the Missionaries of Charity. Born in Macedonia, this frail nun campaigned ceaselessly for the world's poor, particularly in India. By 1979, the movement had 700 shelters and clinics.

In 1971, Mother Teresa was awarded the first Pope John XXIII Peace Prize, in 1979 the Nobel Prize and in 1983 the British Order of Merit. Her achievements and reputation as a living saint attracted world leaders to seek her advice.

In the week ending 9 January 1970, 2,850 people in Britain died from Hong Kong 'flu.

True

The winter of 1969–70 saw a high death toll, due to influenza. The above figure was the worst since 1933, but was much lower than in the major epidemic of 1918, which caused an estimated 20 million deaths throughout the world.

When the New English Bible *was published on 17 March 1970, people protested by not buying it.*

False

There was, in fact, much demand for the *New English Bible*. The Oxford and Cambridge University presses had exhausted their total output of one million copies by the end of the first day it went on sale. They were reprinting it at the rate of 20,000 copies a week. The edition most in demand contained the Apocrypha and cost 35 shillings.

Mary Wilson, the Prime Minister's wife, published a volume of 'Selected Poems' in September 1970.

True

The volume was priced at 12 shillings and caused a stir at the time. People queued to have copies signed by the author. Her husband, Harold Wilson, kept well in the background. She said that now that they were not living at Number 10 Downing Street — Heath defeated Wilson at the polls in June 1970 — she hoped to have more time to write poetry.

PUZZLE 4 *TRUE OR FALSE?*

On 9 February 1971, 18 months after the British Army moved into Northern Ireland, the first soldier was killed.

True

The troops moved into the province in August 1969. The soldier was killed during an attack by gelignite bombs and machine gun fire as his unit moved into the Ardoyne district. Two civilians and five other soldiers were wounded in the incident.

In 1972, Clifford Irving obtained interviews with, and wrote the biography of, millionaire recluse, Howard Hughes.

False

This was one of the great hoaxes of the century. In March 1972, Irving admitted to a New York court that he had fabricated the biography. He had been paid $750,000 by McGraw-Hill, the publishers, for transcripts of 100 supposed interviews. *Time Magazine* had also bought the serial rights. Irving had wrongly assumed that Hughes would not denounce him.

On 5 December 1973, the government imposed a 50mph speed limit on British roads to save fuel.

True

The government also printed ration books in case it became necessary to ration petrol. Some 200 petrol stations closed down because of shortages. This was brought about by the large increase in OPEC's oil prices and the resultant increase in the trade gap.

Measures were introduced to limit non-oil import demands, including tighter hire-purchase and credit controls to help with the gap. The OPEC countries had cut back oil production and increased prices by some 70 per cent in protest at US support for Israel in the Yom Kippur war, and as a warning to other nations. It was an attempt to get policies changed.

TRUE OR FALSE? PUZZLE 4

On 20 March 1974, there was an attempt to kidnap Prince Charles.

False

It was in fact an attempt to kidnap Princess Anne. An armed man drove in front of her car. He fired six shots, but neither Princess Anne nor Mark Phillips, who was with her, was hurt. A bodyguard, the chauffeur, a policeman and a passing taxi driver were wounded.

The man had planned to demand a £1 million ransom. In the event, he fled into St James's Park, where he was arrested.

In a report published by the Forestry Commission in October 1975, it was said that Dutch Elm disease had destroyed 6.5 million elm trees in Britain.

True

The disease, spread by a fungus, was first recorded in Britain in 1867 and was described in the Netherlands in 1919 — hence the name. It is thought to be of Asiatic origin.

A new, more lethal strain of the disease was found in the early seventies — it was thought to have come into the country on logs from Canada. This spread rapidly through the south of England, killing millions of trees, and appeared to be moving north. Individual trees could be protected by fungicides, but they were very expensive to use on a large scale.

The Labour MP, John Stonehouse, was wrongly accused of fraud in 1976.

False

Stonehouse organized an elaborate disappearance by leaving his clothes on a Miami beach. He later turned up in Australia, where he had been using an assumed name and a false passport. He received a seven-year sentence for fraud. His accomplice and mistress, Sheila Buckley, was given a suspended two-year sentence. Stonehouse was once thought to have the potential to become leader of the Labour party.

PUZZLE 4 *TRUE OR FALSE?*

1976 saw the driest summer since records had begun in 1727.

True

Emergency legislation had to be rushed through Parliament because of the serious problems with water supplies. The source of the Thames dried up, and in London it reached its lowest level in living memory. Reservoirs turned into arid plains and local authorities were given power to control many types of water use. Water rationing was introduced in South Wales, south-west England and parts of Yorkshire.

Red Rum won his third Grand National on 2 April 1977.

True

Red Rum was the first horse to win this steeplechase more than twice. He was ridden by Tommy Stack and won by 25 lengths. His previous wins were in 1973 and 1974. He was runner-up in 1975 and 1976. He also became the first horse to win both the English and Scottish Nationals in the same year, 1974. He was withdrawn on the eve of the 1978 National because of a bruised heel and went into retirement.

In March 1979, in a referendum on home rule, Wales voted massively to have its own mini-parliament and Scotland voted against the idea.

False

Wales, in fact, voted massively against having its own mini-parliament. Only 12 per cent said 'Yes' to a Cardiff assembly, 47 per cent said 'No' and the remainder did not vote.

In Scotland there were 33 per cent for an Edinburgh assembly and 31 per cent against it. All this fell well below the 40 per cent acceptability test for home rule.

DO YOU REMEMBER?

Television

There was the outrageous Alf Garnett in 'Till Death Us Do Part'. He was an ageing skinhead with steel-rimmed spectacles, a moustache and the vilest of tempers — a candidate for the psychiatrist's couch, if ever there was one. He voiced the most reactionary impulses and prejudices of the day.

Another popular series was Galsworthy's 'Forsyte Saga'. Some 17 million viewers watched this story on Sunday evenings, and it was popular in America, the Soviet Union and 40 other countries.

'Monty Python's Flying Circus' was full of surreal slapstick. John Cleese clowned about in a nervous manner and maintained decorum in the face of absurdity, as when doing his 'silly walks', devised by a government department in the series. This, too, attracted large audiences and was transferred from BBC2 to BBC1. 1975 saw the creation of the manic hotel manager, Basil Fawlty, in 'Fawlty Towers', another John Cleese success.

'Upstairs, Downstairs' ended in 1975. This was the story of a household in Eaton Place, in which Gordon Jackson played the butler, Hudson, who remained loyal to the class system to the end. Also in 1975, viewers were entertained with the play 'The Naked Civil Servant', from an autobiography by Quentin Crisp. In it, John Hurt played the embattled homosexual.

In 1976, the serial epic based on Robert Graves's 'I Claudius' began. This was an account of the early Roman Empire narrated by the nervous Emperor, played by Derek Jacobi. This year also saw the end of 'Dixon of Dock Green'. Jack Warner, at 80, was still playing Sergeant Dixon after 21 years under the blue lamp, fighting the villains of Dock Green.

1978 saw the introduction of the cantankerous barrister 'Rumpole of the Bailey', played by Leo McKern.

In 1979, the BBC produced 'Tinker Tailor Soldier Spy', adapted from the novel by John Le Carré (1974). It starred Alec Guinness as the mole hunter, George Smiley. The new faces of Rowan Atkinson, Mel Smith, Griff Rhys-Jones and Pamela Stephenson featured in 'Not the Nine O'clock News'.

PUZZLE 5 *WHAT'S THE CONNECTION?*

CAN YOU PUZZLE OUT THE CONNECTION BETWEEN THE FOLLOWING?

George C. Scott
General George S. Patton

The film *Patton* (1970)

The film, *Patton*, in which he played General George S. Patton, won George C. Scott an Oscar nomination. Scott refused the nomination, saying that the awards ceremony was a meat parade that 'degraded his profession'. The film depicted the story of Patton during the Second World War. It pulled no punches and included the infamous incident when Patton accused a shell-shocked private of malingering and struck him. Rod Steiger turned down the role because of his strong dislike of Patton's attitudes and views.

Edward Heath
Morning Cloud
August 1971

The Admiral's Cup

Edward Heath skippered the sloop *Morning Cloud* in the Admiral's Cup race and led the British team to victory. Heath personally took the helm as *Morning Cloud* sailed into Plymouth. *Morning Cloud* lost part of her spinnaker gear off the Scillies and was the last of three British yachts to finish, but all three finished comfortably ahead of the opposition.

Emperor Hirohito
The Queen
October 1971

Emperor Hirohito made a state visit to Britain

When he arrived on the state visit, the Emperor was greeted by a large, but silent, crowd. The Queen was reported to have told him, "We cannot pretend that the past did not exist."

Many people, including former Japanese prisoners of war, protested at the Emperor's visit and called for a boycott of Japanese goods. Hirohito was the first Japanese sovereign to leave Japan in more than 2,000 years.

WHAT'S THE CONNECTION? PUZZLE 5

President de Gaulle
Frederick Forsyth
An assassination attempt

The novel *The Day of the Jackal* (1971)

Frederick Forsyth wrote the novel, which described the attempted assassination of General de Gaulle by a professional hired by the OAS. Most of the characters in the book were real people, thinly disguised. The book was turned into a successful film in 1973. Edward Fox played the killer, code-named 'Jackal'. Other novels by Forsyth in the seventies included *The Odessa File* (1972), *The Dogs of War* (1974) and *The Devil's Alternative* (1979).

Reginald Maudling
John Poulson
A police enquiry in 1972

A financial corruption scandal

Reginald Maudling, who was Home Secretary, resigned because he was chairman of a Poulson company. A police enquiry was set up to investigate allegations of financial corruption in public life. Poulson was an architect engaged in building contracts in the public sector. He was said to have given away more than £500,000 in suits, holidays and flowers to win contracts with councils, health authorities and nationalized industries. Poulson was jailed for seven years.

Glenda Jackson
Cleopatra
Christmas 1974

'The Morecambe and Wise Show'

After winning her second Oscar for her role in the film *A Touch of Class* (1973), Glenda Jackson appeared as a special Christmas guest on the Morecambe and Wise Show in 1974 as Cleopatra. Clips from the appearance have been repeated many times. She won her first Oscar for her role in *Women in Love* (1969).

Richard John Bingham
Lord Lucan
A nanny

Murder

In November 1974, Richard John Bingham, who was the seventh Earl of Lucan, allegedly murdered Sandra Rivett, his child's nanny, attacked his wife and then disappeared. He was well known in London's gaming society as 'Lucky'. In June 1975, although Lord Lucan had not been found, an inquest named him as the killer of the nanny. The Countess told the jury that he had also tried to strangle her. Friends believed that he had committed suicide. His disappearance remains a mystery.

A London flat
Four IRA gunmen
Two hostages

The Balcombe Street Siege

The four IRA men attacked a restaurant in the West End of London on 6 December 1975. Police had been alerted and were waiting for them. The men made a run for it and a gun battle took place. They took refuge in a flat in Balcombe Street and held the occupants, Mr and Mrs Matthews, hostage. The terrorists demanded a safe passage to the Republic of Ireland, but the authorities refused to give in to the demands.

On 12 December, after it became known that a Special Air Services assault team was about to arrive, the hostages were released. Shortly afterwards, the four men gave themselves up.

A fire
A sculptress
Cornwall
21 May 1975

Barbara Hepworth died in the fire

Barbara Hepworth died in a fire at her home in St Ives, Cornwall on 21 May 1975. She was 72. Dame Barbara gained international status as a sculptress. She developed abstract forms in stone or wood. Her public commissions included 'Winged Figure' at the United Nations headquarters in New York.

WHAT'S THE CONNECTION? PUZZLE 5

Harold Wilson
James Callaghan
16 March 1976

Callaghan succeeded Wilson as Prime Minister

Harold Wilson completely surprised his cabinet colleagues when he announced his retirement as Premier and leader of his party on 16 March 1976. He had led the Labour party for 13 years. However, it was not done on the spur of the moment, as he had made the decision in March 1974, when he was returned as Prime Minister. He also told the Queen of his intentions in December 1975.

Laurence Olivier
Dustin Hoffman
A search for diamonds

The film *Marathon Man* (1976)

Olivier played a former Nazi at large in New York, searching for hidden diamonds. Hoffman plays the innocent bystander caught up in events. He is tortured by Olivier, who poses as a dentist and drills into one of Hoffman's good teeth. Apparently, the scene had to be cut somewhat because at the previews too many people in the audience were fainting.

The underground car park in the
House of Commons
An IRA bomb
30 March 1979

Airey Neave

On 30 March 1979, Airey Neave, Britain's opposition spokesman on Northern Ireland, was killed by an IRA bomb as he was leaving the underground car park at the House of Commons in London. As Conservative spokesman on Ulster, he had advocated a tough line on security to combat the IRA and knew he was a possible target.

The Jeremy Thorpe affair

Jeremy Thorpe resigned from the Liberal party leadership on 10 May 1976, because of allegations about his sexual involvement with a male model. On 13 December 1978, magistrates at Minehead committed Thorpe for trial at the Old Bailey. He was accused, with three other men, of conspiring to murder Norman Scott, the male model.

During the trial, in May 1979, Scott told the jury about his alleged homosexual relationship with Thorpe. Scott claimed that Thorpe saw his disclosure about the affair as a threat to his political career.

The trial lasted for 31 days and the jury found Thorpe not guilty of plotting murder or inciting others to kill Scott.

Ayatollah Khomeini

In February 1979, the Ayatollah Khomeini made a triumphant return to Iran after 16 years in exile. From his headquarters on the outskirts of Paris he had managed to mastermind the fall of the Shah of Iran, who fled to Egypt.

Films in the seventies

A Clockwork Orange, the film version of Anthony Burgess's novel, appeared in 1971. It is about a young thug called Alex. He lives in a society set in the future, and is arrested for murder. He is subjected to treatment designed to instil in him an aversion to sex and violence.

Clint Eastwood introduced 'Dirty Harry' in a movie of the same name in 1971. The hero is known as 'Dirty Harry' because he is given all the dirty jobs and because of the dubious methods he uses. The following year, Al Pacino and Marlon Brando appeared in *The Godfather*, which was followed by *The Godfather, Part Two* in 1974.

In 1975, *Jaws* did for sharks what Alfred Hitchcock's *Psycho* did for showers. It was reported in America that in the first six weeks after its release one person in eight had seen it.

Other popular movies towards the end of the decade included *All the President's Men* (1976), *One Flew Over the Cuckoo's Nest* (1976), *Star Wars* (1977), *A Bridge Too Far* (1977), *Close Encounters of the Third Kind* (1977), *Grease* (1978), *Superman* (1978), *The Deer Hunter* (1978), *Apocalypse Now* (1979) and *Kramer versus Kramer* (1979).

FAMOUS PEOPLE CROSSWORD

DRAW THIS CROSSWORD ON A BLACKBOARD, PHOTOCOPY THIS PAGE AND GIVE IT TO
EACH PERSON, OR USE THE CLUES AS A STRAIGHT QUIZ

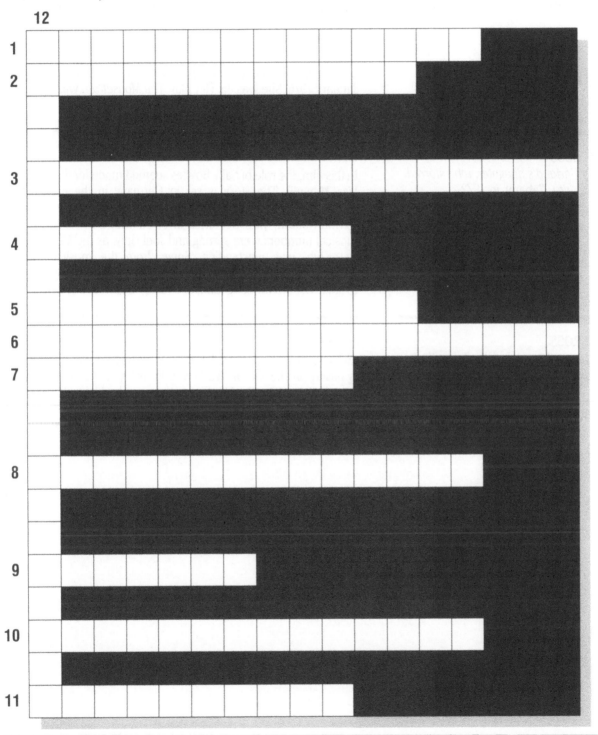

PUZZLE 6 *FAMOUS PEOPLE CROSSWORD*

1 ACROSS
She created the fictional character, Hercule Poirot.

Agatha Christie

Agatha Christie was probably the most successful novelist ever, with world sales exceeding 300 million. The last Hercule Poirot book, *Curtain: Hercule Poirot's Last Case*, was published in 1975. Another memorable character created by Agatha Christie was Miss Marple.

Agatha Christie, the queen of the detective story, died on 12 January 1976. She was 85. Her play, *The Mousetrap*, was in its 25th year at St Martin's Theatre, London.

2 ACROSS
Judy Garland's daughter, who starred in the film, Cabaret, in 1972.

Liza Minnelli

In this film, the role of Sally Bowles seemed made for the talents of Liza Minnelli. The story is set in Germany in the early 1930s. Michael York is her English lover. Helmut Griem plays a homosexual German baron, who becomes involved with both of them. The musical numbers were stirring and Joel Grey, as the MC of the Kit Kat Klub, was outstanding. Songs from the musical include 'Wilkommen', 'Don't Tell Mama', 'Two Ladies', 'Tomorrow Belongs to Me', 'The Money Song' and, of course, 'Cabaret'.

3 ACROSS
He wrote the musical, 'Evita', with lyricist Tim Rice.

Andrew Lloyd-Webber

'Evita' (1978) was another hit musical for Andrew Lloyd-Webber. It is based on the life of Eva Peron. Probably its most memorable song is 'Don't Cry For Me Argentina', sung by Elaine Paige in the opening show. Other extraordinary early successes for Lloyd-Webber were 'Joseph and the Amazing Technicolor Dreamcoat', 'Jesus Christ Superstar' and 'Cats'.

FAMOUS PEOPLE CROSSWORD PUZZLE 6

4 ACROSS
He was elected leader of the Liberal party on 7 July 1976.

David Steel
David Steel succeeded Jeremy Thorpe as leader of the Liberal party. He was the first party leader in Britain to be elected by party supporters outside Parliament, rather than by MPs. In 1977, he entered into a Lib–Lab pact which kept the Labour leader, Jim Callaghan, in power and gave the Liberals a say in government policy.

5 ACROSS
He was pardoned by US President Gerald Ford for his wrongdoing.

Richard Nixon
President Nixon was undone by his own phobia. Convinced that he was being conspired against, he launched a conspiracy of his own, which led to the Watergate affair.

Although a whole series of unethical and illegal acts were revealed concerning Nixon's staff, he stubbornly refused to admit his involvement and tried to conceal the facts. He resigned in August 1974, before Congress could impeach him, and spent the remainder of his years trying to restore his destroyed reputation.

6 ACROSS
He wrote and starred in the boxing film hit, Rocky *(1976).*

Sylvester Stallone
Sylvester Stallone was born in 1946 and raised in Manhattan's 'Hell's Kitchen' neighbourhood. His upbringing was turbulent. He has said: "I wandered through 14 High Schools and five Colleges without getting a degree." He worked in jobs ranging from zoo attendant to a pizza demonstrator, before becoming an actor.

He was reported to have written the screenplay for *Rocky* in three days. It is about an unknown boxer who is given an unexpected chance and rises to the opportunity.

PUZZLE 6 *FAMOUS PEOPLE CROSSWORD*

7 ACROSS

A Russian gymnast who won a gold medal during the 1972 Munich Olympics on the beam and the floor.

8 ACROSS

A US Secretary of State who won the Nobel Peace Prize in 1973 and was known for his shuttle diplomacy.

9 ACROSS

A brutal dictator nicknamed 'Big Daddy' whose eight-year rule in Uganda (1971–9) revolted the world.

Olga Korbut

This waif-like gymnast from the USSR won everyone's heart, proving herself to be a world class entertainer and supreme performer during the Games. As well as the gold medal, she won a silver medal on the bars and shared the team gold. In 1976 she also won a silver medal on the beam.

Henry Kissinger

Between 1973 and 1977, Henry Kissinger's achievements included restoring diplomatic ties between the United States and China, and ending the Vietnam War. He worked tirelessly to find a settlement after the 1973 Israel–Arab war. He also paved the way for Presidential visits between America and Russia and general detente.

Idi Amin

This dictator seized power from Milton Obote in 1971. He was a former army boxing champion and served in the King's African Rifles in Kenya during the Mau Mau uprisings. During his reign of terror, 300,000 died and he expelled Uganda's 70,000 Asian community. He fell from power in 1979, when Tanzania responded to a Ugandan invasion of its territory. He fled to Libya, but was expelled and moved to Jeddah.

FAMOUS PEOPLE CROSSWORD PUZZLE 6

10 ACROSS

She made an underwater swim to save the others in the film, The Poseidon Adventure *(1972).*

Shelley Winters

Her underwater swim was one of the highlights of the film. The script was adapted from a novel by Paul Gallico. A luxury ocean liner is hit by a tidal wave and capsizes, leaving the surviving passengers to find their way out of a ship that has been turned upside-down. Other stars in the film were Gene Hackman, Ernest Borgnine, Red Buttons and Carol Lynley.

11 ACROSS

This blithe spirit who had a 'talent to amuse' was known as 'The Master' and died at his home in Jamaica in March 1973, aged 73.

Noel Coward

Noel Coward was the son of an unsuccessful piano tuner from South London. He began as a child actor in 1910. Gertrude Lawrence, whom he met on a tour in 1913, became his friend and co-star until her death. Coward was an actor, writer and composer. His successes on stage included: 'Hay Fever' (1925), 'Private Lives' (1930) and 'Blithe Spirit' (1941). He wrote the screenplay for the film *Brief Encounter* (1945) and appeared in many films himself.

Later, he perfected a cabaret act, with which he took Las Vegas by storm. He left behind the memory of one of the most ineffable of English men and entertainers.

12 DOWN

This man was expelled from the USSR after he exposed the conditions in Soviet labour camps under Lenin and Stalin by publishing his book, The Gulag Archipelago, *in Paris in 1974.*

Alexander Solzhenitsyn

Solzhenitsyn had held up publication for five years to protect victims whose names appeared in the book. The author first came to literary attention with the publication of *One Day in the Life of Ivan Denisovich* (1962), the story of one prisoner's experience from morning to night. Thereafter, his books had to be published abroad. They included *The First Circle* (1968) and *Cancer Ward* (1968).

In his history of the labour camps he incredibly defied the entire Soviet state. Since then, the treason charges against him have been dropped and he has returned to his homeland.

the 1980s

***T*HE 1980s** may go down in history as the decade which saw a turning-point in the relations not only between countries, but also between people and the natural environment.

When Mikhail Gorbachev became leader of the Soviet Union in 1985, he took a fresh approach to domestic and international affairs. The words 'glasnost' (openness) and 'perestroika' (reconstruction) entered the international vocabulary. Most dramatic of all was the collapse of Communist rule in the East European states in 1989. One after another, the governments of Poland, Hungary, Czechoslovakia, Bulgaria, East Germany and Romania gave way to public demand for democratic reform. The most significant symbol of change was the opening of the Berlin wall, which prompted discussion and fear about the reunification of Germany.

Concern about the environment went to the top of the political agenda. This was spurred by the world's worst nuclear disaster, at Chernobyl in Russia, research into the 'greenhouse effect' and information available about the depletion of the world's ozone layer. It was recognized that this was the time to act to protect the environment.

The Prime Minister, Margaret Thatcher, became a significant figure on the world scene, largely owing to the Falklands conflict with Argentina in 1982. In Britain, 'Thatcherism' went into full swing. The Prime Minister proclaimed a battle against inflation and launched a campaign to regenerate Britain's recession-hit economy. People were subjected to a barrage of propaganda in favour of individual enterprise, the supremacy of market forces and the need for cost-effectiveness. Trade union power was restrained and there was an urgent programme of 'privatization' of nationalized industries. This was praised by some as the way to achieve a new prosperity and condemned by others as a way of creating mass unemployment.

To be 'working class' in the eighties seemed to be old-fashioned and inappropriate in an age when everyone had fitted carpets, televisions, deep-freezes, home computers, cars and so on — or so it seemed for those in work and enjoying these benefits. This, however, was not a true picture. By the end of the eighties unemployment was as bad as it had been in the dark days of the thirties. The difference was that in the eighties unemployment received little sympathetic publicity: life on the dole was best ignored and forgotten. When it was highlighted, it was usually to point out how irresponsible the unemployed were for wanting something for nothing.

WHO DID WHAT? PUZZLE 1

NAME THE PERSON OR PERSONS INVOLVED IN THE FOLLOWING EVENTS

To which Wimbledon tennis champion was John McEnroe referring when, in July 1980, he said: "I wish ... would let someone else have a go at the title, for a change"?

Bjorn Borg

John McEnroe made the statement after being defeated by Borg. It was, in fact, Borg's fifth successive men's title at Wimbledon. However, in 1981, McEnroe managed to beat Borg and win the title himself. Borg retired from tennis in 1983, at the age of 26.

Which British ice skating couple won the European ice skating dance championships in February 1981?

Jayne Torvill and Christopher Dean

Torvill was 23 and Dean 22 when they won this title, which had been in the hands of Russian skaters for the previous 12 years. Later, in February 1984, the pair danced to the rhythm of Ravel's 'Bolero' and won an Olympic gold in Sarajevo. All nine judges awarded the Nottingham couple maximum points for artistic impression.

Which ginger-haired snooker player won the world snooker championship in 1981?

Steve Davis

Steve Davis, from South London, beat Doug Mountjoy 18–12 at Sheffield to win the championship. He was aged 23 at the time. It was the pinnacle of a very successful season in which he had also won the English professional title.

PUZZLE 1 *WHO DID WHAT?*

Which member of the royal family was married on 19 July 1981?

Prince Charles

The Prince of Wales married Lady Diana Spencer, who had been a kindergarten helper at St Paul's Cathedral. Some 750 million viewers world-wide watched the event on television.

The festivities had begun the previous day, when Prince Charles lit the first of a chain of 102 beacons across the British Isles, and thousands watched a fireworks display in London's Hyde Park.

Lady Diana arrived at St Paul's with her father, Earl Spencer, in the glass coach which had been used by King George V at his coronation in 1910. She wore an ivory silk taffeta dress with a 25-foot train. She was accompanied by five bridesmaids and two page-boys.

After the events of the day, the couple appeared on Buckingham Palace balcony and, to the delight of the crowd, kissed. They left for their honeymoon in a landau which had a cluster of balloons attached and a sign which read: 'Just Married'.

Which Irish novelist, who could type only with the toe of one foot, died on 6 September 1981?

Christy Brown

Born with cerebral palsy, Christy Brown was treated like a vegetable until he started to use chalk to draw with his foot. His best-selling novel, *Down All The Days*, which was based on his own life, came out in 1970. Other works included *A Shadow on Summer* (1974) and *Wild Grow The Lilies* (1976). He also wrote poetry. His autobiography, *My Left Foot*, was made into a film in 1989 and starred Daniel Day-Lewis. Christy Brown was 48 years old when he died.

Who played Gandhi in the film of the same name in 1982?

Ben Kingsley

Ben Kingsley is himself Anglo-Indian and his name was Krishna Banji. His father emigrated to England and practised as a doctor in Manchester. To prepare himself for the role, Kingsley tried to live as closely as he could to Gandhi's lifestyle.

The film was directed by Richard Attenborough and cost some £9.5 million to make. In the Academy awards, presented in April 1983, the film won best picture, best director and best actor awards.

WHO DID WHAT? PUZZLE 1

Which pop star enlisted fellow artistes to produce the chart-topping record 'Do they know it's Christmas?', in December 1984?

Bob Geldof

The rock stars were brought together by Boomtown Rats singer Bob Geldof to help the starving refugees of Ethiopia. The singers called themselves 'Band Aid'.

Later, in 1985, Geldof did it again on an international scale and organized two huge concerts — one in Wembley Stadium, the other in JFK Stadium in Philadelphia. More than one-and-a-half billion people in 160 countries watched the concerts on television. Performers included Dire Straits, David Bowie, Mick Jagger and Queen. The stars, who gave both their time and their talents free, raised more than £40 million to help starving people in Africa.

Which 17-year-old became the first unseeded tennis player to win the Wimbledon men's title, in 1985?

Boris Becker

He was also the first German to win the title. To do so, he beat Kevin Curren 6–3, 6–7(4–7), 7–6(7–3), 6–4. In 1984, he had left the tournament in a wheelchair after badly injuring himself.

Which 'Clean Up TV' campaigner launched a furious attack on BBC's soap opera series, 'Eastenders', in April 1987?

Mary Whitehouse

While speaking to the Listeners' Association's annual convention, she claimed the programme's bad language and general portrayal of low morals were a 'peril' to viewers and children. To back up this view, she cited examples of an episode in which two homosexuals embraced as being 'the height of irresponsibility'. She felt that the programme could not be justified, as young children would be watching. Some episodes, she claimed, 'could have torn viewers' sensitivities to shreds'.

PUZZLE 1 *WHO DID WHAT?*

Which British jockey was jailed on 23 October 1987 for three years, after admitting tax evasion totalling over £3 million?

Lester Piggott

This phenomenally successful jockey, who had retired in 1985, was also stripped of his OBE. In 1988, he was paroled and, in 1989, at the age of 54, he applied to renew his jockey's licence and made a brilliant comeback by winning the Breeder's Cup Mile at Belmont Park, New York on Royal Academy.

Piggott is estimated to have ridden over 5,000 winners. This includes a record nine Derby victories.

Which Canadian athlete set a world record in the Olympic 100 metres and was later stripped of his gold medal for drug-taking in Seoul, in 1988?

Ben Johnson

Ben Johnson was initially hailed as a hero when he set the world record, winning the 100 metres final. He was called the fastest man on earth. After being found guilty of using drugs, he flew back to Canada in disgrace. Nine other athletes were also disqualified from the same Olympics after failing drug tests.

Which junior health minister was forced to resign in December 1988 over her claim that most British eggs were infected with salmonella?

Edwina Curry

She resigned after angry protests from farmers over her claim that British eggs were infected with salmonella. Following her statements, the sale of eggs slumped and egg producers demanded compensation from the government. Health experts did agree that Britain faced the worst-ever outbreak of salmonella. Despite this, Edwina Curry was forced to resign.

She had previously earned a reputation for being offensive by making statements such as "Northerners die of ignorance and crisps", "Cervical cancer is the result of being far too sexually active" and "Good Christian people ... will not catch AIDS."

Roy Plomley

This courteous host of 'Desert Island Discs' was a 'regular' on BBC radio, from 1941 until his death in 1985. He interviewed some 1,790 castaways, including Princess Margaret and Mrs Thatcher. No other BBC programme had ever run as long with the same presenter. He was 71 when he died.

Who did the household tasks

Although the position of women at work had generally improved through the outlawing of sexual discrimination and sexual harassment, maternity leave and equal pay, many women still worked part-time in unskilled jobs, earning low wages. Women were still regarded by many men as naturally inferior in the workplace. At home, their place was in the kitchen and doing the housework.

A social trends survey in 1985 revealed that 89 per cent of women did the washing and ironing, 77 per cent prepared the evening meal, 72 per cent did the household cleaning and 51 per cent did the shopping. Only doing the evening dishes was shared equally between partners.

The man getting into the Queen's bedroom

On 7 July 1982, the Queen awoke to find a man sitting on her bed in Buckingham Palace. He was drinking from a bottle of wine he had stolen from the cellars and wanted to talk to her.

The Queen played along until her intruder asked for a cigarette. This gave her an opportunity to summon help. The 30-year-old man, Michael Fagan, was remanded in custody and charged with theft of the wine and trespassing. The incident highlighted the lax security at the Palace.

Reading habits

In 1987, the *Sun* was the most popular newspaper, with a readership of 11.3 million. Its circulation rose between 1971 and 1987 by 33 per cent, aided, no doubt, by large pictures of bare-breasted women on page three. The circulation of the *Daily Mirror* fell by 34 per cent in the same period.

The *News of the World* was the most popular Sunday paper, with a readership of 12.8 million. The *Sunday Mirror* was read by 9.1 million.

The two most popular women's magazines in 1987 were *Woman's Own*, with 4.8 million readers, and *Woman*, with 3.6 million.

CAN YOU LINK THE PERSON NAMED WITH THE BOOK, FILM, MUSIC, SPORT OR SUBJECT?

Salman Rushdie	Sculpture
Paul Hogan	Racing
Mike Hailwood	Rain Man
Mike Tyson	On Golden Pond
Tom Cruise	Cricket
Diego Maradona	Crocodile Dundee
Laura Ashley	Athletics
Zola Budd	The Satanic Verses
Ian Botham	Boxing
Henry Fonda	Motor-cycle racing
Bob Champion	Fashion
Henry Moore	Football

Salman Rushdie

The Satanic Verses (1988)

This novel by Salman Rushdie was publicly burnt at a demonstration by over 1,000 Moslems in Bradford, on 14 January 1989. The title, *The Satanic Verses*, refers to verses ordered to be cut from the Koran by the Prophet Mohammed, which he believed were inspired by Satan. The book was banned as blasphemous in India, Pakistan and Saudi Arabia. Rushdie was brought up as a Moslem and said that the book concerned the struggle between the secular and the religious view of life.

In February 1989, the Ayatollah Khomeini, the Iranian leader, ordered the execution of Salman Rushdie. Rushdie cancelled a planned tour of the USA and went into hiding. His life has remained under threat ever since.

Paul Hogan

Crocodile Dundee (1986)

The Australian comedian Paul Hogan starred as 'Crocodile Dundee' in this film. He was born in 1941, the second of three children of an army sergeant turned postman. Hogan grew up in a working-class suburb of Sydney and dropped out of school at 15. He appeared in a television programme called 'New Faces' in 1972. Later, he had his own programme, 'The Paul Hogan Show', and did advertisements for the tourist board and Foster's lager. Now he is known world-wide.

Mike Hailwood

Motor-cycle racing

Mike Hailwood won nine world championships and 14 Tourist Trophy titles on the Isle of Man circuit. Known as 'Mike the Bike', he retired from motor-cycle racing in 1968 to drive formula one racing cars.

Hailwood died in a car accident two miles from his home in Warwickshire on 23 March 1981. His car collided with a lorry. His nine-year-old daughter died with him. He was aged 40.

Mike Tyson

Boxing

At the age of 20, Mike Tyson became world heavyweight boxing champion when, in November 1986, he beat Trevor Berbick in two rounds in Las Vegas to win the WBC title.

Tom Cruise

Rain Man (1988)

Tom Cruise plays the sharp-dealing brother of an autistic man called Raymond (Dustin Hoffman). This was an attempt by Cruise to be taken more seriously than he had been in his previous films, such as *Top Gun* (1986). In 1989, he went on to give a good dramatic performance in *Born on the Fourth of July*. This was the story of a soldier who had suffered a spinal injury in the Vietnam war.

Diego Maradona

Football

Diego Maradona was the captain of the Argentinian football team when they won the World Cup in June 1986, in Mexico. They beat England in the quarter-final, Belgium in the semi-final and West Germany 3–2 in the final.

In June 1982, Maradona became the most expensive footballer in history when he joined Barcelona in a deal worth $7.7 million. He is 5' 4" tall and usually plays mid-field.

Laura Ashley

Fashion

Welsh-born Laura Ashley started out designing tea-towels on her kitchen table. This grew into a multi-million pound international business, employing over 4,000 people. Her flowery style of clothes appealed widely, as did similarly styled furnishing and wallpaper.

She died, after a fall, at her home in September 1985. She was aged 60.

Zola Budd

Athletics

In January 1984, this 17-year-old South African distance runner beat Mary Decker's 5,000 metres world record. Later, there was controversy when it became known that she was to receive a British passport. This enabled her to beat the ban on South African athletes and made her eligible to run for Great Britain in the Los Angeles Olympic Games in 1984. There were further controversy and recriminations when she ran in the 3,000-metre race in the Olympics and Mary Decker tripped over her heels. Budd ran bare-foot.

Ian Botham

Cricket

Ian Botham was England captain during 1980–81 and was voted man of the series in the 1981–2 Australian tour. In 1984, he took eight wickets in the test against the West Indies. Botham is famous as a batsman, bowler and larger-than-life character who has been involved in many fund-raising events for charity.

Henry Fonda

On Golden Pond (1981)

In this film Henry Fonda played a tetchy elderly man who has difficulty acknowledging the love he has for his fiercely independent daughter (Jane Fonda). Katharine Hepburn plays Henry Fonda's wife.

The part won Henry Fonda his only 'best actor' Oscar in the awards, presented in 1982. He died, after a long illness, on 12 August, the same year. He was born in Nebraska in 1905. He is reported to have said about himself and the parts he played: "I'm not really Henry Fonda. Nobody could have that much integrity."

Bob Champion

Racing

Bob Champion won the affection of the racing public in 1981, when he won the Grand National on Aldaniti. In 1979, after being diagnosed as suffering from cancer, he was given eight months to live. His fight back to health caught the imagination of his supporters. Also, the fact that the horse, Aldaniti — after years of tendon trouble and a broken hock bone — led the field from start to finish added to the occasion.

Henry Moore

Sculpture

Henry Moore worked in wood, bronze, stone and cement and was known for his smooth organic forms. Frequently, he developed variations on the themes of a reclining figure and a mother and child. He often pierced holes through the middle of his figures, enhancing their three-dimensional effect.

He was a miner's son from Castleford, Yorkshire, and said that he enjoyed the 'hard navvying' of working with stone. In 1940, he became an official war artist and drew pictures of people sheltering from air raids in the London underground stations. His work was highly praised around the world. He died on 31 August 1986.

Telegrams

On 19 October 1981, British Telecom announced that it was going to scrap the telegram. By autumn 1982, it was to be replaced by a 'tele-message', which was to arrive by post the day after it was sent. No longer would messages of triumph or disaster be accepted over the Post Office counter. Instead, they would be phoned or telexed. The change-over to the new system involved the loss of some 1,400 jobs.

Neil Kinnock being elected leader of the Labour party

Neil Kinnock became MP for Bedwellty, South Wales, in 1970. From 1974 to 1975, he worked for Michael Foot as personal private secretary. He became a member of the Labour party's National Executive Committee in 1978, and chief Opposition spokesman on education in 1979.

After Labour was defeated in the 1983 General Election and Michael Foot resigned, Kinnock was elected leader of the Labour party on 2 October of the same year. He had an overwhelming majority. Roy Hattersley was his deputy on what was called 'our dream ticket'.

The favourite indoor pastime

Watching television was the most engaged-in pastime of the eighties. In 1987, everyone watched it for an average of 25.5 hours. Those aged over 65 watched for 37.5 hours and the under-15s for 19 hours. Between 9pm and 9.30pm, 41.7 per cent of the population watched television.

The Piper Alpha tragedy

On 6 June 1988, fire engulfed the Piper Alpha oil-rig platform in the North Sea. A series of explosions wrecked the 12-year-old rig, which was located about 120 miles north-east of Aberdeen. Flames shot over 400 feet in the air.

Most of the men who died were asleep. A large number of those who survived escaped by jumping 200 feet into the sea. The extreme heat could be felt up to a mile away by rescuers.

The fire took several days to put out and the talents of the Texas oilman, Red Adair, were recruited to bring it under control. Ironically, the rig had passed a safety regulation test eight days before the disaster.

PUZZLE 3 *WHAT HAPPENED?*

What happened to Daley Thompson in the Moscow Olympics in 1980?

He won the decathlon

In these Olympics, Daley Thompson won the first ever British gold medal for the decathlon. And he won gold again in the Los Angeles Olympics in 1984. Daley's father was Nigerian and his mother Scottish.

What happened to Peter Sutcliffe on 5 January 1981?

He was charged with 13 murders

Sutcliffe, a 35-year-old truck driver, was thick-set, with curly black hair and a short beard. In April 1981, he admitted that he was the Yorkshire Ripper and had attacked and killed 13 women over a four-year period. He also admitted murder attempts on seven other women. At the Old Bailey, he pleaded manslaughter on the grounds of diminished responsibility.

What happened to Pope John Paul II in St Peter's Square, Rome, on 13 May 1981?

He was shot

The incident occurred when Pope John Paul II was driving in his open-top jeep through a crowd of over 10,000 people in St Peter's Square. The Turkish gunman used a Browning 9mm pistol. Four bullets hit the Pope and two women were also injured. The Pope survived a five-hour operation after the shooting.

What happened to the John De Lorean sports car project in Belfast on 19 February 1982?

It went into receivership

John De Lorean had persuaded the state to put £17.5 million into the project in 1978. On 19 February 1982, James Prior, the Ulster Secretary, made it clear there would be no more cash available for the project.

The cars were low-slung, fibre-glass sports cars, which were aimed at the US luxury market. The government had invested the money in the project hoping to boost jobs in Northern Ireland. But De Lorean said in 1982 that the firm needed a further £16–27 million to survive. Speculation, at the time, suggested De Lorean was a con man. This was a picture which seemed to be reinforced when, in October 1982, he was arrested in Los Angeles and charged with possessing cocaine.

What happened to King Henry VIII's flagship, the Mary Rose, in the Solent on 11 October 1982?

Her remains were raised from the sea bed

The ship had been under water in the Solent for 437 years. In 1545, she had sailed out to engage in battle with the French fleet, when she capsized and sank. Prior to 1982, over a period of more than 20 years, a quantity of artefacts and weapons had been raised from the sea bed by divers.

What happened at York Minster on 9 July 1984?

It caught fire

The fire was started by a bolt of lightning. Damage to the 700-year-old Minster was estimated at £1 million. However, most of the cathedral's treasures were saved by clergy.

It was suggested at the time that the fire was linked to the consecration of the controversial Rt. Revd David Jenkins as Bishop of Durham. The Archbishop of York dismissed the divine link as 'ridiculous'.

PUZZLE 3 *WHAT HAPPENED?*

What happened at Bradford City football ground on 11 May 1985?

The main stand caught fire

A total of 46 people died when fire engulfed the stand. The blaze was started, it was thought, when a cigarette or match ignited rubbish which had accumulated under the seats. The fire spread rapidly and burst into an inferno. Many of those who died were trapped at the back of the stand because exit gates and turnstiles had been padlocked. The team had just been promoted to the Second Division and were playing Lincoln City.

What happened at Westminster Abbey on 23 July 1986, involving a member of the royal family?

Prince Andrew got married

Prince Andrew married Miss Sarah Ferguson, known as 'Fergie'. They became the Duke and Duchess of York, a title conferred by the Queen. Prince Andrew was born in 1960 and is the third child of Queen Elizabeth II and Prince Philip.

What happened to the stock market on 19 October 1987?

The bottom fell out of it

Ten per cent was wiped off the value of public-quoted companies in London by a wave of selling. It was the worst day for shares this century.

The crash followed a Wall Street panic the previous Friday and also heavy selling in Tokyo. The collapse was blamed by analysts on the US budget and trade deficits and rising interest rates. The date, 19 October, became known as Black Monday.

What happened to Prince Charles in Switzerland on 10 March 1988?

He was nearly killed by an avalanche

Prince Charles and his friends were skiing near Klosters, in Switzerland, when an avalanche caught them. One member of the royal party, Major Hugh Lindsay, a former equerry to the Queen, died and a woman, Mrs Palmer-Tomkinson, was injured. Later, in June 1988, a magistrate blamed the royal party for the avalanche.

What happened in Tiananmen Square, Beijing, China, on 4 June 1989?

The People's Liberation Army shot demonstrators

Hundreds of thousands of students, supported by many people from other walks of life, gathered in Tiananmen Square to show their dissatisfaction with the country's leadership and to demand democratic reform. On 4 June, the government decided to end the protests by sending in the People's Liberation Army to disperse them. The soldiers fired into the crowds indiscriminately. More than 2,000 people are thought to have been killed and many thousands injured.

What happened to the Guildford Four on 19 October 1989?

Their murder convictions were overturned

Three of the Guildford Four, Gerard Conlon, Carole Richardson and Patrick Armstrong, were set free after serving 14 years in prison. The fourth, Paul Hill, remained in custody for another case, in which he was implicated, to be resolved.

All four had been convicted of pub bombings in 1975. The court of appeal found that the convictions had been based on police lies and fabricated evidence. Police notes about interviews had been rewritten, altered and suppressed.

Films of the eighties

In 1981, two little-known actors, Ben Cross and Ian Charleson, had a big success with *Chariots of Fire*. It is the story of two top athletes who ran in the 1924 Olympics. Cross played Harold Abrahams, a Jewish Cambridge student, who runs because he is snubbed racially and wants to prove something. Charleson played Eric Liddell, a devout Scottish missionary, who refuses to run because his event takes place on a Sunday.

Arnold Schwarzenegger (born in Austria) came to the screen in 1982, starring in *Conan the Barbarian*. *E.T. The Extraterrestrial* (1982) told the story of a friendship between a young boy and a 600–800-year-old creature from outer space, with a catch phrase, "E.T. phone home".

Also in 1982, Dustin Hoffman was 'Tootsie', an actor who dons women's clothes in order to get a good part. Jack Nicholson and Shirley MacLaine starred in *Terms of Endearment* in 1983. *Gremlin* was one of the delights of 1984. Other 1984 successes were *Police Academy* and *Romancing the Stone*.

Michael J. Fox became a hit in the film *Back to the Future* (1985), which was aimed mainly at young people. At the other end of the scale, Don Ameche starred in *Cocoon* (1985). Tom Cruise spent weeks studying the gestures and body language of a top flying team to make *Top Gun* (1986). The film made him into a superstar. Michael Douglas became a *Fatal Attraction* (1987) for Glenn Close — this was a study of a vengeful woman destroyed by sexual obsession. In 1987, *The Last Emperor* told the story of Pu Yi, who was the last of the old Chinese imperial line.

The decade ended with *Batman* (1989). Jack Nicholson hammed it up as 'The Joker', Batman's arch enemy. There was also Robin Williams in *Dead Poets' Society* (1989) and Billy Crystal in *When Harry Met Sally* (1989). In the latter film, in the funniest sequence of the story, Meg Ryan conclusively demonstrates — in a crowded restaurant — that an orgasm can be faked.

TRUE OR FALSE? PUZZLE 4

The 1980 Olympic Games were held in Los Angeles.

False

The 1980 Olympics were held in Moscow. It was the 1984 Olympics which were held in Los Angeles. The games in Moscow were distorted by the absence of America, West Germany and Kenya in protest over the Soviet Union's invasion of Afghanistan. The Soviet Union countries retaliated by not attending the Los Angeles games.

After being shot in the chest on 30 March 1981, Ronald Reagan said to his wife: "Honey, I forgot to duck."

True

The 70-year-old President was leaving a Washington hotel when his attacker, John Hinckley III, fired six shots. One shot hit the President in the chest and lodged in his left lung. Three other men were also wounded. Later, when his wife, Nancy Reagan, visited him in hospital he made the joke about not ducking — quoted from an old film.

Oxford won the Boat Race on 4 April 1981, using the first-ever woman cox.

True

Susan Brown steered her crew to a decisive victory, finishing eight lengths in front. She trained some six hours a day over a period of six months, both on the water and in a gym, for the event. She was 22 and came from Honiton in Devon.

PUZZLE 4 TRUE OR FALSE?

Lord Carrington resigned as Foreign Secretary on 5 April 1982 because of the Falklands affair.

True

When he resigned, he said: "I accept responsibility for a great national humiliation." He was referring to the Argentinian invasion of the Falklands. Two other Foreign Office ministers also resigned: Humphrey Atkins and Richard Luce.

Lord Carrington felt that, because his efforts to find a diplomatic solution to the crisis had failed, he had to resign as a matter of honour.

Sir Ralph Richardson often rode his motor-cycle round Regent's Park with his parrot on his shoulder.

True

Sir Ralph Richardson was not only a great actor but a great English eccentric. Until his death on 10 October 1983, at the age of 80, he would frequently give his parrot an outing by riding his motor-cycle around Regent's Park.

Richardson's most notable part was in 1945, when he played Falstaff in Shakespeare's Henry IV. He refused to repeat the performance in further productions.

Clive Sinclair launched a new type of aqua-car which could travel on land or sea in 1985.

False

Clive Sinclair invented the C5, which was his answer to the traffic problem. It was a low-slung, lightweight, single-seat, battery- and pedal-powered tricycle. It had a range of 20 miles before the battery needed recharging, ran on a washing machine motor and was capable of travelling at 15mph. It cost £399. Sir Clive said that, by the end of the century, 'the petrol engine would be a thing of the past'.

The public were not convinced about his invention and treated it as something of a joke. On 29 March 1985, production of the C5 electric tricycle was suspended and on 14 October 1985 his company called in the receiver.

TRUE OR FALSE? PUZZLE 4

In 1985, just over half the population in Britain smoked cigarettes.

False

According to a government survey, only one person in three still smoked. The figure for men had the more dramatic fall — from 52 per cent in 1972 to 36 per cent in 1985. Women smokers fell from 41 per cent to 32 per cent over the same period. Also, the survey indicated that those who did smoke were smoking less.

Jeffrey Archer resigned as Deputy Chairman of the Conservative party in order to become a full-time novelist, in October 1986.

False

Archer did resign, but it was because of newspaper allegations that he had attempted to pay a prostitute to go abroad to avoid a scandal. He said that he had to resign 'for lack of judgement'. He denied ever meeting the prostitute, but said that he had fallen into a trap to get him to offer her money. Later, in July 1987, Archer won a libel action against the *Daily Star*.

On 13 February 1987, a property the size of a small room was on sale in London for £36,500.

True

The property was 5' 6" (1.67m) wide by 11' 0" (3.35m) long and was recommended for someone who liked eating out, as there was no cooker. It did have a single radiator, a shower, a wash basin and a lavatory. An added attraction to its buyer was its location — opposite Harrods.

PUZZLE 4 *TRUE OR FALSE?*

The 1987 American film, Three Men and a Baby, *was a remake of the 1985 French hit,* Three Men and A Cradle.

True

This very popular film starred Tom Selleck, Steve Guttenberg and Ted Danson as the three men left holding the baby. The picture was directed by Leonard Nimoy, who is better known as Mr Spock in the 'Star Trek' television series and movies.

On 26 March 1989, the Bishop of Durham, the Rt. Revd David Jenkins, got into trouble for saying: "We really do not know what the resurrection of Jesus Christ from the dead means."

True

He made the statement during an Easter address in Durham Cathedral. Later, in a television interview, he expanded on the remark and said that the spiritual aspect was what mattered, not 'the revival of a corpse'. Eight MPs called for his resignation over the affair.

Nigel Lawson, the Chancellor of the Exchequer, was sacked by Mrs Thatcher on 26 October 1989.

False

Nigel Lawson resigned. In the morning he had had a disagreement with Mrs Thatcher. He felt that his position had become untenable as he was constantly being undermined by Mrs Thatcher's economic adviser, Professor Sir Alan Walters. Lawson tried to get the Prime Minister to agree to sack Walters by the end of the year. She did not comply and Lawson resigned. In his letter he said: "Successful conduct of economic policy is possible only if there is full agreement between the Prime Minister and the Chancellor of the Exchequer."

John Major was immediately appointed as successor to Nigel Lawson.

Teenagers retaining the right to contraceptive pills

A high court judge, on 26 July 1983, refused to rule that it was illegal for doctors to supply contraceptive pills to girls under 16 without their parents' consent. Anti-pill campaigners were very disappointed and protested that they no longer had the right to protect their own children.

The Hitler diaries

The German magazine, *Stern*, *The Sunday Times* and Lord Dacre, formerly Hugh Trevor-Roper, were convinced the 60 diaries were authentic. Times Newspapers refused to confirm that they had paid £1 million for the right to publish extracts.

On 6 May 1983, the 'Hitler diaries' were declared by experts to be fake. A few days later, on 14 May, the alleged author of the diaries (Konrad Kujan) gave himself up to the police and, on 27 May, Gerd Heidemann, the reporter who 'discovered' the 'Hitler diaries', was arrested. It was all a great hoax.

The storm of the decade

In October 1987, the south of England was battered by winds which gusted to over 100mph, causing damage estimated between £100 and £600 million. Houses and hotels were destroyed from Cornwall to East Anglia. Roads and railway lines were blocked by thousands of trees torn out of the ground by the winds. Many areas were without electricity for several days.

The London fire brigade dealt with over 6,000 emergencies within 24 hours. Kew Gardens lost a third of its trees, some of which could not be replaced. Hospitals were filled with casualties injured by flying slates and other debris. At least 17 people died.

Peter Wright

Peter Wright, a former MI5 man, wrote his memoirs and found himself in a long battle with the British government, who wanted to ban publication of his book, *Spycatcher*. The government lost its battle on 13 October 1988, when the House of Lords rejected efforts to bar any mention of the book in Britain's media. Peter Wright argued that evidence of MI5's lawbreaking, presented in the memoirs, justified the book's publication.

PUZZLE 5 *WHAT'S THE CONNECTION?*

CAN YOU PUZZLE OUT THE CONNECTION BETWEEN THE FOLLOWING?

Special Air Service
Iranian Embassy, Knightsbridge
5 May 1980

The SAS stormed the embassy

A group of Iranian terrorists calling themselves the 'Group of the Martyr' occupied the Embassy on 30 April 1980. They demanded the release of 91 fellow Arabs imprisoned by the Ayatollah Khomeini regime in Iran. They threatened to kill their 26 hostages and blow up the embassy unless the demands were met. The negotiations dragged on until the terrorists finally asked only for a safe passage out of Britain. However, on 5 May they shot dead two of the hostages.

Later that day, the SAS stormed the embassy from all angles. Within a few minutes five of the six gunmen were dead and the surviving hostages were released.

John Lennon
New York
8 December 1980

Mark Chapman shot John Lennon

The shooting took place outside the Dakota building in New York. John Lennon and his wife, Yoko Ono, were returning from a recording session and walking into the building when he was shot five times. Chapman, it was said, had stalked Lennon for three days and obtained his autograph the day he shot him.

Argentina
Britain
April–June 1982

The Falklands war

The conflict began when, on 2 April, Argentinian forces invaded the Falkland Islands. Britain responded by getting together a large task force and setting sail. It took three weeks to travel the 8,000 miles to the islands.

The British forces recaptured South Georgia by the end of April. During May they established a bridgehead on East Falklands and the advance began to Goose Green and Darwin. On 14 June, the Argentinian forces surrendered to the British commander. The conflict cost 254 British and 750 Argentinian lives.

WHAT'S THE CONNECTION?

Orgreave
Police
Mineworkers
29 May 1984

Pitched battles between police and mineworkers

The miners had been on strike for 12 weeks when the police turned up for the first time in full riot gear. Some 28 miners and over 40 policemen were injured in the police charges. Later, the police blamed the violence on the presence of Arthur Scargill, the NUM president.

At the time, the coal board was insisting on talks about cutting output by four million tons a year and the closure of up to 20 uneconomic pits, with the loss of over 20,000 jobs.

Death of a black woman
North London
October 1985

Race riots

The woman, Cynthia Jarrett, died of a heart attack during a police search of her flat. Another woman, Cherry Grose, was shot. Afterwards, several hundred black youths rioted. Police charges were stopped by petrol bombs, stones and setting ire to cars. Over 200 police were injured.

On 15 January 1987, a policeman was cleared of criminal charges of shooting Cherry Grose and on 19 March, Winston Silcock, a ringleader of the riots, was jailed for life for murdering PC Keith Blakelock during the riots.

Chernobyl
A fire
16 April 1986

A nuclear accident

This accident, which started with a fire, was the worst ever nuclear disaster. The Soviet Union was slow to react and only acknowledged the accident four days after it happened, when high radiation levels were detected in Sweden. To avoid meltdown, the damaged reactor was sealed with concrete. However, restrictions were placed on the sale of animal products in many countries, as tests showed levels of radiation were well above normal in grazing animals.

PUZZLE 5 WHAT'S THE CONNECTION?

Zeebrugge
Herald of Free Enterprise
6 March 1987

The ferry, *Herald of Free Enterprise*, capsized

The tragedy happened outside the harbour walls of the Belgian port of Zeebrugge. More than 500 people were on board. The accident caused the death of 184 people. Many acts of heroism were reported on the night of the rescue. The ship had gone to sea with her bow doors open. This allowed an inrush of water to the open car deck, causing the ship to capsize.

A Pan American jumbo jet
Lockerbie
22 December 1988

An air crash

The Pan American flight 103, a Boeing 747, was on its way from Frankfurt, via Heathrow, to New York. A terrorist bomb, hidden in a radio-cassette player, exploded on the plane, causing it to fall 31,000 feet, crash across a major road and plough into the town of Lockerbie, in Scotland. Some 40 houses were destroyed in the impact. Many of the 270 who died were Americans returning to the USA for Christmas.

Frank Bruno
Las Vegas
25 February 1989

World heavyweight title fight

Mike Tyson had little trouble in beating the courageous Frank Bruno in this world heavyweight title fight. Bruno was knocked down in the first round, but bravely continued until the referee stopped the bout in the fifth.

WHAT'S THE CONNECTION? PUZZLE 5

Hillsborough
Liverpool
Nottingham Forest
15 April 1989

Hillsborough football tragedy

During the final of the FA cup at Hillsborough Stadium in Sheffield, between Liverpool and Nottingham Forest, 95 Liverpool fans were crushed to death. Many others were injured.

The police had ordered a gate to be opened to allow a tightly packed crowd of fans in to watch the match. People at the front became trapped behind fixed steel fences designed to stop hooligans invading the pitch. Many of the dead were teenagers.

The Marchioness
River Thames
20 August 1989

***The Marchioness* sank in the river Thames**

The accident happened in the early hours. A birthday party was in full swing, with an estimated 150 people on board, when the vessel was struck by the 2,000-ton dredger, *Bowbelle. The Marchioness* keeled over and sank, and 51 of the party-goers died.

Berlin
10 November 1989

East Berliners swarmed into West Berlin

At the stroke of midnight on 9 November 1989, East Berliners began swarming into West Berlin. The Berlin wall lost its significance as people poured through the checkpoints and climbed the wall. Many danced on top of it and chipped great chunks loose. East Germans were at last free to leave the country and join their relatives in the West.

During the 28 years that the wall had stood, at least 75 people died trying to escape. It had been erected in August 1961 to stop refugees fleeing to the West.

The move towards home ownership

The Conservative government's Housing Act 1980 gave tenants of council houses the right to buy their homes after three years. This was reduced to two years in 1984. Sales between 1980 and the end of 1987, encouraged by the discounts offered, reached more than one million.

By the end of the eighties the proportion of working-class people owning their own homes was nearly 50 per cent. Those who did were generally more comfortable, had telephones, microwave ovens, video recorders and so on; 66 per cent of households had a car by 1988.

In stark contrast to this, at the end of 1985, nearly 15,500 known households were in temporary accommodation such as bed and breakfast, short-life dwellings and hostels. By 1988, the number had risen to 32,000. This figure did not include people who were sleeping rough.

Your favourite leisure activities

Some 65 per cent of men and 47 per cent of women liked going to the local pub for a drink. The next most popular activity was going out for a meal. To accommodate this, many more public houses began to open their own restaurants or serve bar meals.

There was a big revival in cinema going. Admissions rose from 58 million in 1984 to 75 million in 1987 — a 29 per cent increase. Families were put off going to football matches by hooliganism, drunkenness, swearing and the abuse of players. Between 1971 and 1987, attendance at football matches fell by 36 per cent. Families watched it on television instead.

The Greenham women

In August 1989, eight years after women began maintaining an anti-nuclear protest outside the Greenham Common air base, they watched the first cruise missiles being removed and flown back to America. The women had maintained their protest through summer and winter, taking every opportunity to make their presence felt and influence the removal of the missiles.

FAMOUS PEOPLE CROSSWORD

DRAW THIS CROSSWORD ON A BLACKBOARD, PHOTOCOPY THIS PAGE AND GIVE IT TO
EACH PERSON, OR USE THE CLUES AS A STRAIGHT QUIZ

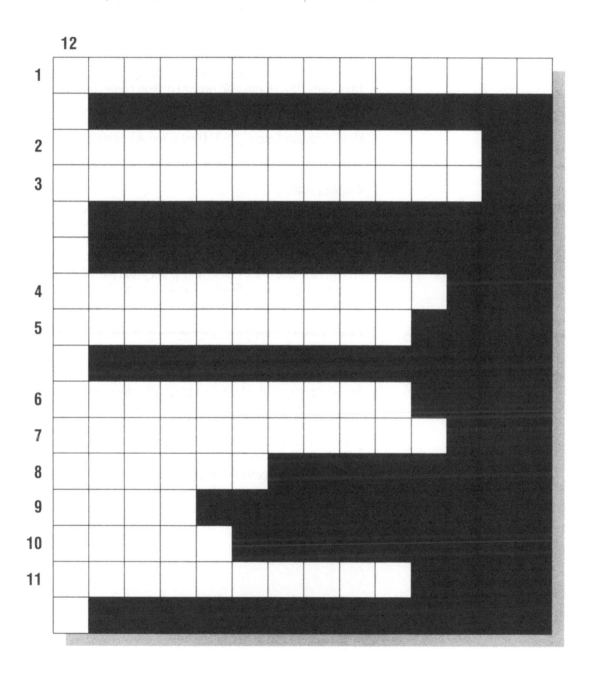

PUZZLE 6 *FAMOUS PEOPLE CROSSWORD*

1 ACROSS
This 'Wacko' rock star played at Wembley Stadium on 16 July 1988.

Michael Jackson

Michael Jackson, often referred to by the Press as 'Wacko Jacko', started singing lead with the Jackson Five and has become one of the most mass-marketed celebrities ever. He has made television and cinema commercials for Pepsi and his reclusive manner of living has fuelled many rumours about an odd lifestyle.

In 1982, seven singles from his album, 'Thriller', made the top 10 records. The album sold over 40 million copies and has become the biggest-selling solo album of all time. The seven singles were 'Billie Jean', 'Beat It', 'Wanna Be Startin' Somethin'', 'The Girl is Mine', 'Human Nature', 'PYT' (Pretty Young Thing) and 'Thriller'.

2 ACROSS
He won the Booker prize in 1986 with his novel, The Old Devils.

Kingsley Amis

Once known as one of the 'angry young men', when his first novel, *Lucky Jim*, came out in 1954, Kingsley Amis won the Booker Prize with a novel about old age. Other novels he has written include *The Anti-Death League* (1966), *Ending Up* (1974), *Jake's Thing* (1978), *Hide-and-Seek* (1980) and *Stanley and the Women* (1984).

Amis was born in South London, became a university lecturer and has been a jazz enthusiast. He was awarded the CBE in 1981.

3 ACROSS
He was Indiana Jones.

Harrison Ford

There were three films in which Harrison Ford played Indiana Jones. *Raiders of the Lost Ark* (1981) tells the story of a search for the Ark of the Covenant. *Indiana Jones and the Temple of Doom* (1984) sees the archaeologist–adventurer in an Indian Maharajah's palace, beneath which is the 'Temple of Doom'. Indy, in conflict with the Nazis, seeks the Holy Grail in *Indiana Jones and the Last Crusade* (1989). Sean Connery plays Indy's father in this film.

FAMOUS PEOPLE CROSSWORD PUZZLE 6

4 ACROSS
The Trade and Industry Secretary who resigned over the Westland affair in January 1986.

Leon Brittan

Leon Brittan resigned under pressure from influential Conservative MPs, following his admission that he had authorized the leaking of a letter criticizing Michael Heseltine while he was Defence Secretary. Ten days previously, Heseltine had resigned 'on a point of honour' and had marched out of a cabinet meeting. The affair concerned a conflict of viewpoints over the future of the Westland helicopter company.

5 ACROSS
He succeeded Ronald Reagan as President of the USA in November 1988.

George Bush

George Bush, the Republican candidate, was the first sitting Vice-President of the USA to win a Presidential election since 1936. He defeated Michael Dukakis, the Democratic candidate, winning 54 per cent of the vote.

6 ACROSS
In 1981, he co-founded the Social Democratic Party.

Roy Jenkins

Roy Jenkins, together with Shirley Williams, David Owen and William Rodgers, formed the new Social Democratic party. The four former cabinet ministers criticized the Labour party for drifting towards extremism. Jenkins became leader of the new party, but resigned after the general election of 1983.

7 ACROSS

Playing a New York detective in Die Hard (1988) made him into a big-screen star.

8 ACROSS

The surname of a Hampshire man who commentated on cricket for 35 years, until he retired in September 1980.

9 ACROSS

She was once married to, and sang with, Sonny Bono.

Bruce Willis

Bruce Willis was John McClane in this thriller, set in a California tower block. A group of hostages are held in one of the upper storeys by a gang of terrorists. The detective, accidentally trapped in the building over Christmas, proceeds to interfere with the terrorists' plans.

Arlott

John Arlott's voice had become synonymous with the radio broadcasting of cricket. On his last appearance, he commentated on the last session of the centenary match at Lord's. As he left the commentary box, both the crowd and the players applauded him.

Cher

Cher was born, part-Armenian and part-Cherokee Indian, in California in 1946. Her full name was Cherilyn La Pierre Sarkisian. At the age of 16 she moved in with — and later married — Sonny Bono, making a number of hit records with him. When she left him, her career lost direction until she went in for straight acting. She was Meryl Streep's lesbian friend in *Silkwood* (1983) and then made *Mask* (1985), playing the tough biker lady, 'Dusty Dennis', who was the mother of a disfigured son.

FAMOUS PEOPLE CROSSWORD PUZZLE 6

10 ACROSS
The surname of a cheeky chat show host from Blackburn, who rivalled Michael Parkinson.

11 ACROSS
In January 1987, her publishers said all new editions of her 'Noddy' books would have the traditional black golliwogs replaced by neutral gnomes.

12 DOWN
He became the new leader of the Soviet Union on 11 March 1985.

Harty
Russell Harty was a schoolmaster for six years, before he became familiar to listeners on Radio 3. He then graduated to television arts programmes and chat shows and, in the eighties, did seaside specials. Audiences loved his cheeky manner, his style of interrupting guests and his unpretentiousness. In one programme, Grace Jones boxed his ears. He died on 8 June 1988, after a long struggle with hepatitis.

Enid Blyton
Critics said that her books were full of ageism, sexism and racism. Macdonalds, her publishers, responded by making changes to her books. Many people, who had read and loved the books, were appalled and felt that the publishers were giving way to ideological purity. They believed that altering books in this way would destroy favourite classics.

Mikhail Gorbachev
At 54, Gorbachev was the youngest member of the Politburo and the only member to hold a degree. At first he believed that the USSR's difficulties could be solved by discipline and strict leadership. By 1987, he had changed his mind and had begun working to make the Soviets into democratic bodies. He ended the cold war and withdrew from Eastern Europe. He will probably be remembered as the leader who was responsible for the disintegration of the USSR.

Related Products . . .

*For Product Safety Concerns and Information please contact
our EU representative GPSR@taylorandfrancis.com Taylor & Francis
Verlag GmbH, Kaufingerstraße 24, 80331 München, Germany*

T - #0001 - 270225 - C0 - 254/202/11 - SB - 9780863883484 - Gloss Lamination